I0528877

Praise for BE THE PROTAGONIST

"In beautiful and inspiring language, the author captures the essence of thousands of years of wisdom from Ayurveda and meditation and integrates that into the stage of life to inspire the reader to become the protagonist of their own story. This book will resonate with seekers of knowledge and offers practical tips and resources to enhance mind, body, and spirit wellbeing."

—*Sheila Patel, MD; Chief Medical Officer, Chopra Global*

"I loved reading BE THE PROTAGONIST. It was a transformative experience. As someone deeply vested in mind-body wellness and Vedic philosophy, I was immediately captivated by the book's unique approach to self-growth.

I'm particularly impressed by how Maria integrates the theatrical concept of *protagonism* into everyday self-improvement practices. It is a touch of genius that adds an engaging narrative to the quest for personal evolution.

One thing I appreciated was the way Maria effortlessly converses with the reader. She encourages active participation in our own transformation.

In a world saturated with self-help guides, BE THE PROTAGONIST rises like the morning sun, casting a beautiful glow on the path to real true evolution, and self-realization."

—*Rashmi Schramm, MD, NBC-HWC*

"Think of the people you just feel good being around. They embody physical health, mental clarity, and a sense of play and purpose. Maria Schaedler-Luera is one of those people and in BE THE PROTAGONIST, she shares how this way of being is not by accident, but by design. This enlightening book deconstructs three practices - ayurveda, meditation, and theater - and succinctly outlines their interconnectedness and the empowering role they can play in creating a healthy body, a clear and focused mind, and a script to become the playwrights of our own lives."

—*Sean Layne, Founder, Focus 5, Inc.; International Arts Integration Company*

"BE THE PROTAGONIST is an enjoyable, engaging, and transformative roadmap to self-discovery. Maria Schaedler-Luera's clear explanations and relatable examples make even the most complex concepts accessible. This book is a valuable guide for all levels of self-development and an essential resource for understanding your unique mind-body constitution, establishing a meditation practice, and embracing your true self through the lens of theatrical expression. BE THE PROTAGONIST is a must-read for anyone seeking a comprehensive and innovative path toward enhanced well-being and self-awareness."

—*Denise 'Yashoda Ma' O'Dunn, Founder, Balance & Bliss Ayurveda & Yoga; Florida Academy of Ayurveda*

"BE THE PROTAGONIST is an insightful read as Maria allows us into her own in-depth process and transformation of identity and relationship to the world. This book also gives gentle guiding of strategies and useful approaches for the reader to engage for all three practices. We are invited to find our own story, identity, and relationship to our communities.

Maria takes us into each practice, weaving and making connections. In these complex times, this book is offering support of balance and harmony that is so needed. As each of us negotiates a very stressful and unpredictable world, BE THE PROTAGONIST is all about *possibility*!

I loved reading this book and highly recommend it. Whatever your role or roles in life are, this book is accessible to wherever you might find yourself."

—*Priscilla H. Sanville, PHD Professor Emerita,*
Lesley University

"Maria Schaedler-Luera shares her journey as a dedicated and insightful student of three different disciplines, while weaving in her powerful insights from years of careful study and practice. Her special art is the passionate synthesis of her experience into the great play of life, and the generous invitation for all of us to step fully into our own roles as keener observers and dynamic actors - as the protagonist in our own lives."

—*Max Roberts-Zirker, Executive Director,*
Shambhala Meditation Center of Boston

BE THE PROTAGONIST

How Ayurveda, Meditation, and Theater
Can Transform Your Life

Maria Schaedler-Luera

Copyright © 2023 by Maria Tereza Schaedler-Luera

All rights reserved.

Published by Ibis Books, 2349 Hyde Park Street, Sarasota, FL, 34239.

No portion of this book may be reproduced in any form without written permission from the publisher or author, except as permitted by U.S. copyright law.

This publication is designed to provide accurate and authoritative information in regard to the subject matter covered. It is sold with the understanding that neither the author nor the publisher is engaged in rendering legal, investment, accounting or other professional services. While the publisher and author have used their best efforts in preparing this book, they make no representations or warranties with respect to the accuracy or completeness of the contents of this book and specifically disclaim any implied warranties of merchantability or fitness for a particular purpose. No warranty may be created or extended by sales representatives or written sales materials. The advice and strategies contained herein may not be suitable for your situation. You should consult with a professional when appropriate. Neither the publisher nor the author shall be liable for any loss of profit or any other commercial damages, including but not limited to special, incidental, consequential, personal, or other damages.

Contents

Foreword

When I first met Maria Schaedler-Luera, we were part of a team creating a training program for parents and educators. I remember watching her contribute to the planning discussions, and all the while I had this strong and undeniable sense of calm. It was present not only when she spoke but also when she was simply listening to others. It intrigued me. How was it that her mere presence elicited such a positive emotion from me? I would later find out exactly why that was, and why—as I like to say—I decided I wanted to be on her bus.

As an avid student of human behavior, it made sense that early in my life I entered the field of social work. But my passion for acting could not be silenced. Even though I had worked professionally as an actor on and off for years, I later went back to school and earned a Master of Fine Arts degree in professional actor training. What I discovered was that both disciplines required me to be an ardent observer of people—myself included. I needed to understand what motivates us, what inspires us, and, most of all, why we seemed to have such difficulty changing behaviors that didn't serve us.

During the three-year program in graduate school, what I was learning and continually practicing was how to... *pay attention.* In acting terms, I was learning how to be fully present. How to live truthfully moment to moment. How to listen actively and resist the temptation to manipulate outcomes. It wasn't called mindfulness, but that's very much what it was. The more I practiced, the better I got.

As I continued to marvel at Maria's impact on me, I suddenly realized... it was her *mindfulness* ringing so clearly in those early meetings I had with her. She was so fully present, and in such a calm, loving, nonjudgmental way. Her energy was palpable and contagious. I wanted to know more about this amazing woman and what I could learn from her.

What I discovered was that Maria, like you and I, had made a deep, unwavering commitment to ongoing and continual personal improvement. She had traveled extensively and explored diverse cultures and the teachings of masters of many disciplines. She investigated, researched, and continually questioned how one can live the fullest, most meaningful, and healthiest life possible. She immersed herself in Ayurveda, mindfulness, meditation, and, yes, theater. And she discovered this magical place where these three disciplines converge. I have also studied all three teachings, but this is the first time I have ever seen how they so beautifully complement, enhance, and track each other. We all understand the power of perspective, and Maria's perspective is tremendously comprehensive. It's like she floated out light years to see the broadest, most inclusive picture possible. Her work truly is groundbreaking.

I believe many of us have studied what it takes to achieve personal fulfillment. We have probably encountered some of the same answers again and again. It's not that we don't know what to do. The challenge is that we don't always do what we know. Maria, however, took massive action as she traveled her path. She not only applied what she was learning, she also began to teach others. She asserts on her website (www.ato mica-arts.com) that her mission is to "Close the gap between knowledge and experience." She is doing just that, and in a unique and masterful way.

I invite you to join me on Maria's bus as she shares insights, information, and activities that can truly transform your life. Let's take this trip together while we learn to be the hero in our own life and the protagonist of our own story. It promises to be a very rewarding journey.

Linda Larsen, BSW, MFA
®CPAE Hall of Fame Keynote Speaker
Author, *12 Secrets to High Self-Esteem*

www.lindalarsen.com

Introduction

I am my life's protagonist.

One of my earliest memories dates back to when I was six or seven years old, enjoying summer vacation. I was standing on a beach in Brazil, my birthplace and childhood home. As I basked in the warm sun, I saw a cruise ship passing far out on the water. I had never seen anything like it!

It was too far away for me to distinguish all the details. However, I vividly recall a massive red flag with a blue cross. The pattern was unfamiliar to me. My family told me that the ship hailed from Norway, or as we say in Portuguese, "Noruega."

Hearing about this foreign place, I felt a sense of purpose wash over me like a wave from the wake of the ship itself. I needed to know more. I can still see myself standing on the beach, gazing at the ship and declaring, "I want to go to Noruega. One day, I will live there!"

That moment sparked a fascination with foreign countries, and I eagerly looked forward to the day when I would be old enough to venture out and explore distant lands.

During my high school years, I stumbled upon an opportunity to embark on an adventure to France through an international student exchange program. Through this program, I would have the privilege of living with a host family who would welcome me into their home for a year as I attended public school. The application deadline was days away, and I had only the weekend to persuade my parents that it was time for me. I tried to be confident and resolute. Fortunately for me, my parents were supportive of my aspirations, and within two whirlwind days I had secured their signatures and all the necessary documentation.

The day my family dropped me off at the airport for my trip to Paris, I was brimming with excitement and enthusiasm, oblivious to how my mother and older sister were struggling to contain their emotions and hold back their tears. My eagerness and anticipation were all-consuming. I didn't look back once.

In the three decades since my first trip to France, I have immersed myself in a lifestyle of exploration and learning, equally comfortable in the roles of both traveler and student. I have been an immigrant, and I have become a naturalized US citizen. I have lived and studied abroad and encountered people from all walks of life. A few years ago, I even had the chance to visit "Noruega" with my parents, husband, and children. I no longer have plans to move there, but it was deeply meaningful to finally visit the far-off land that had captured my childhood imagination.

To this day, I relish opportunities to learn about other cultures and ways of life, to accumulate knowledge and expand my understanding of the world. I've discovered that the more you learn, the more you are capable of learning. But I've also discovered that knowledge, though intangible, can weigh heavily.

A few years ago, a conversation with a friend left a profound impact on me. He shared an analogy of a traveler, a wanderer with a backpack, on a quest to explore new worlds and uncover the meaning of life. At each destination, the traveler would immerse herself in the local culture, learn about their perspectives, and collect books as souvenirs, placing them in her backpack before moving on to the next place. However, after many stops, the weight of her backpack had become so burdensome that it impeded her progress.

The solution was clear. The traveler needed to lighten her backpack. And so she began, at each stop, to take out one book, share its knowledge with those eager to listen, and leave the book behind before continuing on her journey. She repeated this process until her backpack was light enough to once again travel with ease.

This analogy of the backpacking traveler resonated deeply with me. Like the traveler, I have eagerly sought new experiences and accumulated knowledge along the way. But that knowledge comes with weight, and at times it can become overwhelming, hindering one's progress. So, again like the traveler, I have cultivated the skill of sharing knowledge with others, which is not only beneficial for them but also lightens my load.

As an immigrant, I have always viewed the world through the eyes of an observer, eager to learn from those around me. Yet I also understand the temptation to assume the role of the perpetual student, clinging to the safety of learning instead of embracing the risk of sharing. So, with this book, I intend to risk by reflecting on the knowledge I have accumulated so far, organizing my thoughts and reflections, and sharing them with you. I hope to not only create more space in my life and make my backpack lighter, but that my experiences—much like that Norwegian cruise ship in the distance did for me—will capture your imagination and inspire you to your own new discoveries.

There is, however, one key discovery I hope above all to share, and it revealed itself to me as I began putting this book together. I realized that all of my various roles—immigrant, traveler, student, observer—were facets of one singular and all-encompassing role: that of *protagonist*.

What does it mean to be the protagonist of one's own life? Being the protagonist means choosing to engage instead of simply observing. Being the protagonist means taking charge of your narrative instead of allowing circumstances to dictate it. Being the protagonist means becoming aware and then maintaining awareness.

It means you insist upon being the pilot and not the co-pilot merely along for the ride in your own life.

This book reflects the protagonist I have been, the protagonist I am becoming, and the protagonist I hope to be. This journey is powered by the intersection of three subjects that have become integral to my life: Ayurveda, Meditation, and Theater. And in this book, I will show you how to apply them so that you too may become your life's protagonist.

This book is my attempt to contribute to our collective knowledge exchange. It draws on ancient wisdom, while also creating and sharing new knowledge and meaning.

Note that my book is not an in-depth guide to these arts and sciences. There are already many resources available on the subjects. (I highly recommend books such as *Ayurveda: The Science of Self-Healing: A Practical Guide* by Dr. Vasant Lad, *Total Meditation: Practices in Living the Awakened Life* by Deepak Chopra, and *Games for Actors and Non-Actors* by Augusto Boal.) Rather, this book explores the interconnection between these pillars of wisdom and how I have applied them in my life.

The one word that sums up how Ayurveda, Meditation, and Theater intertwine—like strands of DNA—is *observation*. Ayurveda is referred to as the "Science of Life," but another way to think of it is "The Art of *Observing* Life." Meditation is a technique for cultivating attention, and you can also think of it as "The Art of *Observing* Ourselves." Theater is a collaborative art form that reenacts real or imagined events, typically on a stage in front of an audience. And as my mentor Augusto

Boal used to say, it is truly "The Art of *Observing* Human Actions."

But observation is only the first step, the means to the end. As you practice the art of observing—life, ourselves, and human actions—you will discover you are building and strengthening your awareness. Only when you become aware can you then act as the protagonist of your life.

Ayurveda emphasizes the importance of being aware of our body and mind, and how they are affected by our lifestyle choices and the surrounding environment. Meditation is a practice that cultivates awareness of our thoughts, emotions, and sensations in the present moment. And theater is an art form that requires us to be fully present and aware of our surroundings, other actors, and the audience.

I have organized this book into four chapters. Chapter One explores Ayurveda and its guiding principle: the interconnection of all things. Chapter Two dives into Meditation and the benefits of slipping beyond thoughts into fields of silence. Chapter Three examines how Theater is a mirror that reflects the human experience, including the many roles we play in life. And Chapter Four then introduces the concept of "Lila," which ties together all three core subjects and shows how to become your life's protagonist through the holistic use of your five senses to deepen your observation and strengthen your awareness.

Lila comes from the Vedas, India's oldest books of wisdom, and can be interpreted as "the Divine Play" or "the Game of

Life." Lila emphasizes our experiences are the manifestation of consciousness. This perspective allows us to view the entire world as a stage, as Shakespeare so eloquently put it in *As You Like It*. We are all actors in the Play of Life, whether or not we realize it. It is when you realize it, and then accept it, that you are then free to claim your role as protagonist.

On stage, actors are highly aware of the language they use, the feelings and relationships of their characters, and their character's journey. However, how many of us are truly aware of the language we use and hear day to day, as well as the wants, desires, and needs of each of the multiple roles we play, much less those of our "co-stars" and "scene partners"?

By applying and integrating the principles explained in this book into your life, you can achieve transformation. Ayurveda, Meditation, and Theater encourage us to reflect on who we are as the protagonists of our own lives, who we aspire to become, and can help us unlock our full potential.

Through observation of life, yourself, and human actions, you can not only become aware of your ability to act, but then also change what you dislike about your life. Each of us is the protagonist in our own story, with the power to shape our reality through our beliefs and actions. But so often we live our lives on autopilot, without awareness, simply reacting to events and circumstances as they come our way instead of taking an active role in determining our path and direction.

This book provides the inspiration to rehearse and envision the future you desire. Even if you can't control the weather, you can fly with purpose and intention. You can change your environment. You can alter the plot of your story. You can impact the world.

All the world's a stage,
And all the men and women merely players;
They have their exits and their entrances;
And one man in his time plays many parts...
                                        —William Shakespeare

Ayurveda
The Art of Observing Life

The Interconnection of All Things

One birthday a few years ago, I gave myself a gift: a solo trip to a Meditation Retreat in California. Being a parent of two young children, the idea of a peaceful weekend filled with silence, rest, rejuvenation, and sleep sounded perfect to me.

During the retreat, as I delved deeper into the practice of meditation and self-discovery, the teacher instructed us to follow an Ayurvedic lifestyle. I had no clue what the term meant and remember jotting it down in my notes. Little did I know that this experience would be a turning point in my life. It was the beginning of a transformative journey.

About 5000 to 6000 years ago, sages in India created Ayurveda, a sophisticated and powerful mind-body health system. Long before modern medicine provided scientific evidence for the mind-body connection, Ayurveda revealed this foundational interconnection and continues to be one of the most significant, powerful, and practiced mind-body health systems worldwide.

As a child growing up in the 80s, I had a deep interest in archaeology, probably because I was a little obsessed with Indiana Jones. While I eventually learned the difference between fiction and reality, my enthusiasm for exploring ancient things and stories persisted throughout my life. When I discovered Ayurveda and its millennia-long lineage, I became captivated and couldn't wait to learn more.

The word "Ayurveda" derives from Sanskrit and means "the science of life" or "the knowledge of longevity." Its foundational principle is that health and wellness depend on a delicate balance between the mind, body, and spirit, and that we can achieve this balance through various treatments and practices.

Ayurveda focuses on preventing and treating actual, underlying illnesses by promoting balance in the body, rather than merely treating symptoms. This holistic approach includes dietary recommendations, herbal remedies, massage, yoga, meditation, and other natural therapies.

Although picking up a book and learning more about Ayurveda was tempting, I didn't want simply to fill up my backpack. I wanted to go on an adventure. I wanted to immerse myself in an experience and uncover all its secrets. Something about this ancient system called to me. So I decided to become certified in Ayurveda. After two years of rigorous study, I proudly became an Ayurvedic Health Counselor in the United States.

Navigating life is challenging enough on its own, pandemic or not. Wouldn't it be great if there was a manual to help us navigate it better? Well, the manual may not be perfect, but it exists as Ayurvedic knowledge. Ayurveda, as the science of life or the "Art of Observing Life," has not only helped me understand my existence but also offered practical tools to enjoy life, improve its quality, prioritize self-care, approach others with greater compassion, and even become a better mother.

I was eager to continue my adventure and made plans to travel to India. However, the outbreak of Covid-19 and subsequent lockdowns forced me to postpone my plans until a little over a year ago. Although I was disappointed, I also discovered that Ayurveda was already a part of my life. During those trying times, Ayurveda proved invaluable in helping me make sense of what was happening and providing me with the tools I needed to navigate the situation with grace and compassion.

Ayurveda encompasses a vast body of wisdom grounded in many principles. However, the most impactful principle for me has been recognizing *the interconnection of all things*. We are not merely a collection of atoms and molecules, but an integral part of the infinite field of intelligence. This concept is rooted in the Vedas, which are among the earliest literary records of any civilization and are revered as the most sacred books of India. These texts offer spiritual insights related to every facet of life and continue to inform and guide seekers of all backgrounds.

According to Ayurvedic philosophy, everything in the universe, from stars to stingrays, is comprised of five elements: ether, air, fire, water, and earth. In humans, these elements come together in different combinations to create the three doshas, or body-mind types.

Doshas are not just physical traits but also mental and emotional tendencies, which can be affected by our environment, diet, and lifestyle choices. These interconnections of elements mean our individual bodies are microcosms of the universe.

We will inspect the elements and the doshas soon, but first I want to go back to the idea of Ayurveda as the art of observing life. Most of us have learned in science classes that the universe as we know it was created during the Big Bang. Physics and math point to the universe starting as a single point that expanded and stretched to what we see today. And it is still expanding.

But I often wonder: that single point! What was it and how did it get there? I don't remember ever talking about that in science class.

According to the Vedas, that single point was an infinite field of intelligence, or you might call it pure consciousness. An eternal, silent field, which holds the potential for everything and, out of which, everything arises. Various traditions and religions call this field by other names, such as The Absolute, Brahman, God, or Energy.

I grew up Catholic, but my relationship with Catholicism has always been complex, and I've never fully identified with it. The Vedic understanding of the world's creation resonates with me much more deeply than the lessons I learned in catechism. I find it more comfortable to refer to the infinite field of intelligence as "pure consciousness," but you are free to use whatever terminology feels right to you.

According to ancient wisdom, pure consciousness is timeless, existing in an eternal now and representing pure awareness. At some point, pure consciousness began to move within itself, generating friction. This friction produced vibrations, sounds, and ultimately, according to the Vedas, the sacred sound "OM."

Following this tradition, the universe did not start with a Big *Bang,* but a Big *OM.* OM is the Primordial Sound of the Universe. The first vibration, the first word. "In the beginning there was the word," as many of us may be familiar with, and the word according to the Vedas was OM. Everything in the universe is comprised of vibration and energy, and the sound of OM represents the underlying unity of all things.

All Ayurvedic literature available to us, from its earliest interpretations to modern texts, is based on the Samkhya philosophy of creation. The old sages in India who wrote the Vedas discovered this knowledge through meditation and observation of nature. The Samkhya philosophy, which was written by the Indian sage Kapila, is one of the oldest interpretations of the Vedas. Kapila outlines twenty-four principles of manifestation from the subtlest and finest element (pure consciousness) to the grossest elements, essentially explaining how all matter evolved in this Big OM.

I will not get into the details of all twenty-four principles, but I do want to highlight the last part of Kapila's theory, which focuses on the five great gross elements (ether, air, fire, water, earth) that make up the very foundation of life. These five elements of life—Pancha Mahabhutas in Sanskrit—represent the energetic forces that exist within all forms. In order to understand life from an Ayurvedic perspective and create balance, we have to understand these elements, their qualities, and how they manifest in our lives.

The Five Elements

Ether

Ether is the first element and the most difficult to analyze and describe. This element is also referred to as Space. It is the essence of emptiness. Ether emerges from the primordial space, from which vibration emanates. It comes from the Big OM. Ether is cold, light, immobile, formless, and impossible to contain.

In the human body, Ether is associated with all our hollow spaces: intestines, blood vessels, bladder, and lungs.

In terms of our senses, Ether is associated with sound and the sense of hearing. Sound vibrations travel through space—through Ether—and have a profound effect on the body and mind. This is why Ayurvedic treatments use music and sound therapy to balance the doshas and promote healing.

In nature, Ether is associated with Winter, after the leaves have fallen, and the earth is empty and cold.

In the cycle of life, Ether is associated with death when the body disintegrates and all that remains is our spirit. We come from spirit and go back to spirit.

Air

From Ether originated the second element, Air. Sometimes called Wind, Air has similar qualities to Ether except that it is mobile. Unlike Ether, Air moves. It is dynamic, but also light, cold, dry, and formless.

In the human body, Air controls breathing, feeds the cells with oxygen, and helps give movement to our biological functions. It keeps our blood circulating, thoughts and nerve impulses flowing, and joints moving.

In terms of our senses, Air is associated with the sense of touch, as the movement of air creates the sensation of touch. Therefore, in Ayurvedic treatments, the sense of touch is often used to balance the air element. This can include practices such as abhyanga (a form of warm oil massage) and marma therapy, which involves the stimulation of specific points on the body to promote healing.

In nature, Air is associated with Fall. The air is cooler, and there is a sense of movement and transition as the leaves fall.

In the cycle of life, Air represents our old age, the period between our most productive stage of life and the last years of our life.

Fire

As Ether transformed into Air, that movement created friction, and that friction generated heat. From that heat comes Fire, the third element. The principle of Fire is transformation. Fire is hot, light, dry, and sharp. By itself, fire is not immobile or mobile. It needs air to give it direction.

Just like the sun generates energy for our planet, Fire generates energy. In the human body, fire manifests in our digestion, perception, ideas, intellect, and understanding.

In terms of our senses, Fire is associated with the sense of vision. The transformational energy of fire allows us to see and understand the world. Therefore, in Ayurvedic treatments, the sense of vision is often used to balance the fire element. This can include practices such as trataka (a form of gazing meditation) and eye exercises to promote eye health.

In nature, Summer is the season of Fire with its warmer, longer days.

In the cycle of life, Fire is associated with our most productive years, from puberty until we transition to old age.

Water

Water is the fourth element, and it is formed from Ether, Air, and Fire. Water represents cohesion. It is cool, stable, heavy, moist, and flowing. Water comprises at least 60% of the human body.

In terms of our senses, Water is associated with the sense of taste, because the taste of water is the most fundamental of all tastes. In Ayurvedic treatments, the sense of taste is used to create balance. This can include practices such as mindful eating and using herbs and spices to enhance the flavor of food.

In nature, Spring is the season of Water, when the frozen water melts and flows from mountains to rivers.

In the cycle of life, Water represents the years of our learning to prepare for life. It's the time of our lives before puberty.

Earth

The fifth and final great element is Earth. All elements are born from Ether and contained in Earth. Earth represents solid matter and the structure of the Universe. It gives form to our bodies and all of creation. Earth is cool, stable, heavy, dry, rough, dense, and hard.

In terms of our senses, Earth is associated with the sense of smell, as the fragrance of the earth is the most fundamental of all smells. In Ayurvedic treatments, the sense of smell is often used to balance the Earth element. This can include practices such as aromatherapy and the use of herbal incense to create a grounding and stabilizing environment.

In nature, late Winter and early Spring represent Earth, when the environment is dry, static, solid, and dormant.

In the cycle of life, Earth represents our time in the womb, when our basic structure is being formed.

The Doshas

Elements do not exist on their own. They relate, interconnect, and combine in different ways. The secret to making sense of how to live life and make better choices, according to Ayurveda, is to understand the connections between elements. The various combinations of these elements create the framework for three vital principles in Ayurveda called doshas, also known as bioenergies or body-mind types.

Vata

Vata is the combination of Ether and Air. Together, they create the energy of movement. Vata regulates all movement activities in the body, both mental and physiological.

In terms of the physical body, Vata governs movement, including breathing, circulation, and elimination. When the Vata dosha is in balance, it promotes healthy movement, flexibility, as well as mental clarity, enthusiasm, and creativity. But an imbalance in Vata can lead to issues such as joint pain, constipation, dry skin, anxiety, insomnia, and digestive problems.

Ayurvedic treatments for balancing the Vata dosha include practices such as warm and nourishing foods, daily self-massage with warm oils, and calming yoga or meditation practices. Using warming and grounding herbs such as ginger, cinnamon, and ashwagandha can also be helpful in balancing the Vata dosha.

Pitta

Pitta is the combination of Fire and Water and represents the energy of heating or metabolism. Pitta governs all the biochemical changes that take place in our bodies, regulating digestion, absorption, simulation, and body temperature.

In terms of the physical body, Pitta governs digestion and metabolism, including the production of digestive enzymes and hormones. When the Pitta dosha is in balance, it promotes efficient digestion, healthy skin and metabolism, and a sharp intellect. An imbalance in Pitta can lead to issues such as acid reflux, ulcers, hormonal imbalances, inflammation, skin rashes, and anger or irritability.

Ayurvedic treatments for balancing the Pitta dosha include practices such as consuming cooling and soothing foods, practicing calming yoga or meditation, and avoiding exposure to hot temperatures. Using cooling and soothing herbs such as aloe vera, coriander, and fennel can also be helpful in balancing the Pitta dosha.

Kapha

Kapha combines Water and Earth and represents the energy that forms the body structure, the glue that holds the cells together. Kapha provides us with strength, vigor, and stability.

In terms of the physical body, Kapha governs structure and stability, including the formation of tissues and organs. When the Kapha dosha is in balance, it promotes healthy tissue formation, strong immunity, healthy joints, and a calm and loving disposition. However, an imbalance in Kapha can lead to issues such as excess mucus, water retention, weight gain, lethargy, and emotional attachment.

Ayurvedic treatments for balancing the Kapha dosha include practices such as consuming light and dry foods, daily exercise, and stimulating yoga or meditation practices. Using warming and stimulating herbs such as ginger, cinnamon, and black pepper can also be helpful in balancing the Kapha dosha.

Prakruti / Vikruti

All three doshas exist inside every human, but one dosha is usually primary, one is secondary, and the third is least present. This means each person has their own particular pattern of energy, their own individual combination of physical, mental, and emotional characteristics that make up their original constitution. (You can identify your own unique constitution by taking the questionnaire at the end of this chapter.)

How do we come by our unique body-mind types or doshas? During conception, each one of us receives a specific combination and proportion of Vata, Pitta, and Kapha based on the genetics, diet, lifestyle, and current emotions of our parents. This "secret recipe" of doshas defines our constitution and nature.

Our doshas are also influenced by our dharma. Dharma refers to a person's life purpose or duty. Each individual has a unique dharma that aligns with their constitution and nature. Understanding one's dharma is essential to achieving optimal health and well-being.

In Ayurveda, our inherent constitution and nature—our "secret recipes"—are called Prakruti. My Prakruti, which is Pitta-Kapha, was passed down to me from my parents according to Ayurvedic principles. It's important to note that my Prakruti is constantly influenced by external factors such as the weather, my sensory experiences, my diet, my digestion, the quality of my relationships, and my surroundings. These external factors often disrupt the balance of my original nature, which in turn affects my overall health.

Being healthy does not mean having equal amounts of all doshas and elements. Instead, it means maintaining the balance of our original doshas. Since we are all unique, what creates balance for one person may not work for another. As we go through life and face different conditions such as weather, diet, stress, emotions, and abundant or insufficient exercise, the balance of the doshas in our mind-body system fluctuates. Any altered state of the doshas is called Vikruti and reflects our current state of health. When our Vikruti is close or equal to our original state or Prakruti, we are in a balanced state and experience good health.

Initially, comprehending the elements and doshas might appear daunting, but once we recognize our distinct body-mind type, life makes more sense. Once I identified myself as a Pitta-Kapha, I came to better understand my inclinations, what makes me happy, and what throws me off balance. Prior to studying Ayurveda, I made instinctive decisions and lifestyle choices that occasionally suited me, but lacked mindfulness. At other times, I made decisions that were fitting for other people in my life, but were not right for me. Now I find myself consistently able to make intentional and effective choices, and not just for myself. By understanding my two daughters' individual body-mind types, I can recognize and cater to their unique requirements and help them maintain balance. Practicing Ayurveda has made me a better mother.

Like Increases Like, Opposites Balance

In Ayurveda, the principle of "Like increases Like" states that substances or qualities that resemble a particular dosha tend to amplify that dosha in the body. If someone with a Pitta predominant constitution (Fire and Water elements)—like my younger daughter—consumes spicy and acidic foods rich in the fire element, her Pitta dosha is likely to increase. When you combine fire with fire, it results in more fire, which can lead to symptoms like heartburn, skin rashes, and irritability.

In contrast, the Ayurvedic principle of "Opposites Balance" suggests that qualities or substances opposite to a specific dosha tend to decrease or balance that dosha in the body. In the example of my Pitta predominant daughter, if she consumes cooling and calming foods like cucumber and mint, it balances the Pitta dosha and reduces symptoms such as skin irritations, acidity, and inflammation.

These principles also extend to mental and emotional states. For instance, a person experiencing anxiety and restlessness (Vata dosha) may find relief by engaging in calming, grounding activities like meditation or yoga, while stimulating activities like vigorous exercise could increase their Vata. Similarly, when someone is feeling angry (high Pitta), it's often recommended that they "cool down." Splashing cold water on the face can ease some of the emotional effects of anger. It's not a foolproof remedy, but I have tested it with my children and found it helpful.

In Ayurveda, the goal of treatment and prevention is to maintain balance among the doshas. Balance can be achieved through a variety of methods, including diet, lifestyle modifications, herbal remedies, and mind-body practices. If you understand the principles of "Like increases Like" and "Opposites Balance," you can make informed choices about your health and well-being, and create a lifestyle for yourself that promotes balance and optimal health.

Identifying your dosha is key to knowing yourself. Your dosha provides clues for what you should eat and what you should address when your energy gets out of whack. The more you know about what may cause certain reactions or tendencies, the easier it will be to balance them. It's like having a map for your hero's journey. When we set sail to a new place, if we don't have a map, we are likely to find ourselves in tough situations for which we did not prepare. Having a map eases the journey and makes it more enjoyable. The Ayurvedic map helps us understand the cycles of life and nature, which activities will aggravate our doshas, and which activities, foods, smells, colors, climates, and daily rituals will balance us.

Maintaining this awareness of how everything interconnects is one of the best tools I have ever encountered in my journey of becoming the protagonist.

Observing and Understanding Life

The interconnectedness of all things is not just a philosophical concept, but a practical approach to health and wellness that emphasizes balance and harmony with the world. The Ayurvedic approach to health and wellness reflects this interconnectedness. Rather than treating isolated symptoms, Ayurveda considers the whole person and their environment, identifying physical, mental, and emotional factors that may impact their health. This concept clarified for me during the pandemic.

According to Ayurveda, a pandemic like COVID-19 can be understood in terms of imbalances in the doshas. The spread of the virus can be seen as a manifestation of an excess of the Kapha dosha, which is associated with stability and structure. Kapha imbalance can lead to congestion, stagnation, and accumulation of toxins in the body, which can create a fertile ground for viral infections to thrive.

Besides the Kapha imbalance, the pandemic can also be seen as a manifestation of imbalances in other doshas. For example, the stress and anxiety caused by the pandemic can aggravate the Vata dosha, which is associated with movement and can lead to nervousness, anxiety, and insomnia. Similarly, the inflammatory response triggered by the virus can aggravate the

Pitta dosha, which is associated with metabolism and can lead to inflammation, fever, and other symptoms.

Ayurveda also recognizes the impact of our actions on the environment and the interconnectedness of all living beings. This is why the practice emphasizes living in harmony with nature, including eating seasonally and locally grown foods, using natural and sustainable resources, and minimizing waste and pollution.

The Vedas are incredible. Not only do they explain how the Universe and Life started, but they also gave us a manual on how to live that life.

Included in that manual, along with Ayurveda, is its sister science, Yoga. I refer to Yoga in this book not as the body poses and exercises that we know in the West as Asanas. I refer to the true meaning of Yoga: "union." Yoga is the return of our body-mind to the infinite field of intelligence or pure consciousness. Because pure consciousness is silent, Yoga is the settling of the mind into silence. We will talk more about this in the next chapter, Meditation.

If Yoga is the tool to go into silence and the practice that helps us develop our awareness to achieve enlightenment, then Ayurveda is the tool to help us care for the being that is on this journey of enlightenment. Ayurveda gives us time and quality of life. It allows us to live a healthy and long life so we can continue on our path toward enlightenment.

Ayurveda has another unique feature that sets it apart from other systems of medicine. It is written in poetry and song. The original knowledge in the Vedas, which helps us comprehend our human potential and the essence of life, is expressed in beautiful verses. It is *musical*.

Research suggests that engaging in music can promote harmony between the right and left hemispheres of the brain. So it should not surprise us that the ancient sages from India imparted their wisdom about life in a form that promotes harmony and balance.

By adopting an Ayurvedic perspective, we can see the interconnectedness of all things and how they influence each other. This new understanding can help us make sense of our lives and find meaning in our experiences. We may find that we can't see the world in any other way now, because everything makes much more sense. We will become more aware of the factors that are influencing our health and well-being and make choices that support balance and harmony.

Ultimately, Ayurveda teaches us that balance is not something we find in life, but something we actively create. This new way of seeing and being in the world can lead to greater peace, happiness, and fulfillment in our lives.

Dosha Questionnaires

The following questionnaires can give you some insight into your Prakruti and Vikruti. Please note that while these questionnaires are a helpful start, a complete Ayurvedic consultation with a qualified practitioner is recommended for fully understanding and determining your doshas, as well as for devising a personalized lifestyle plan. [1]

Part I: Prakruti - Your Natural Constitution

When answering the questionnaire for your Prakruti, consider your natural tendencies, preferences, and behaviors. For instance, "Naturally, normally I am..." Additionally, to gain accurate insights into your inherent constitution, it is advisable to answer questions based on your pre-puberty age.

You can mark more than one option if you feel it accurately reflects your characteristics.

BODY FRAME
a. Thin and bony
b. Medium and muscular
c. Large and sturdy

SKIN TYPE
a. Dry, rough, or thin
b. Sensitive, oily, or warm
c. Thick, oily, or cool

---

1. To download a free PDF copy of these questionnaires, visit https://atomica-arts.com/dosha-questionnaires/

Hair

a. Dry, brittle, or frizzy

b. Fine, thin, or balding

c. Thick, wavy, or oily

Eyes

a. Small, dry, or restless

b. Sharp, penetrating, or sensitive to light

c. Large, attractive, or calm

Teeth

a. Crowded, crooked, or weak

b. Medium, sensitive, or sharp

c. Large, white, or strong

Nails

a. Thin, brittle, or cracked

b. Soft, flexible, or yellowish

c. Thick, strong, or smooth

Appetite

a. Low, variable, or irregular

b. Strong, excessive, or acidic

c. Moderate, steady, or heavy

Thirst

a. Low, variable, or absent

b. Strong, excessive, or frequent

c. Moderate, steady, or occasional

Digestion

a. Slow, irregular, frequent gas or burping

b. Strong, regular, can eat full portions without discomfort

c. Moderate, heavy feeling after eating

Elimination

a. Irregular, constipated, or dry

b. Frequent, loose, or soft

c. Slow, steady, or heavy

Sleep

a. Light, variable, or insomnia

b. Moderate, sound, or restless

c. Heavy, long, or oversleeping

Energy

a. High energy, restless, easily exhausted

b. Strong, sharp, moderate endurance

c. Low, steady, high endurance

MIND

a. Restless, anxious, or fearful

b. Sharp, critical, or competitive

c. Calm, patient, or forgiving

MEMORY

a. Quick, but easily forgetful

b. Sharp, but easily distracted

c. Slow, but long-lasting

ADAPTABILITY

a. Resistant, stubborn, or slow

b. Adaptable, flexible, or impulsive

c. Cautious, thoughtful, or deliberate

RESISTANCE TO ILLNESS

a. Low, often sick

b. Moderate, occasionally sick

c. Strong, rarely sick

Part II: Vikruti - Your Current Imbalance

When answering the questions for your Vikruti, consider any current imbalances or disturbances in your doshas. For example, "Currently, I am..." Focus on your present state of being, considering any recent changes or fluctuations in your physical, mental, and emotional experiences.

Please mark more than one option if multiple characteristics apply to your current condition.

BODY FRAME
a. Thin and bony
b. Medium and muscular
c. Large and sturdy

SKIN TYPE
a. Dry, rough, or thin
b. Sensitive, oily, or warm
c. Thick, oily, or cool

HAIR
a. Dry, brittle, or frizzy
b. Fine, thin, or balding
c. Thick, wavy, or oily

EYES
a. Small, dry, or restless
b. Sharp, penetrating, or sensitive to light
c. Large, attractive, or calm

Teeth
a. Crowded, crooked, or weak

b. Medium, sensitive, or sharp

c. Large, white, or strong

Nails
a. Thin, brittle, or cracked

b. Soft, flexible, or yellowish

c. Thick, strong, or smooth

Appetite
a. Low, variable, or irregular

b. Strong, excessive, or acidic

c. Moderate, steady, or heavy

Thirst
a. Low, variable, or absent

b. Strong, excessive, or frequent

c. Moderate, steady, or occasional

Digestion
a. Slow, irregular, frequent gas or burping

b. Strong, regular, can eat full portions without discomfort

c. Moderate, heavy feeling after eating

ELIMINATION

a. Irregular, constipated, or dry

b. Frequent, loose, or soft

c. Slow, steady, or heavy

SLEEP

a. Light, variable, or insomnia

b. Moderate, sound, or restless

c. Heavy, long, or oversleeping

ENERGY

a. High energy, restless, easily exhausted

b. Strong, sharp, moderate endurance

c. Low, steady, high endurance

MIND

a. Restless, anxious, or fearful

b. Sharp, critical, or competitive

c. Calm, patient, or forgiving

MEMORY

a. Quick, but easily forgetful

b. Sharp, but easily distracted

c. Slow, but long-lasting

Adaptability

a. Resistant, stubborn, or slow

b. Adaptable, flexible, or impulsive

c. Cautious, thoughtful, or deliberate

RESISTANCE TO ILLNESS

a. Low, often sick

b. Moderate, occasionally sick

c. Strong, rarely sick

Results

After completing the questionnaire, you can calculate your Prakruti and Vikruti by counting the number of responses you gave for each category (Vata, Pitta, and Kapha) in Part I and Part II.

For Part I, if you answered most questions (a) then you are more Vata-predominant. If (b) then Pitta-predominant. If (c) then Kapha-predominant.

For Part II, you can determine your current imbalance by identifying any significant differences between your Part I and Part II responses. Any changes in your dominant dosha between Part I and Part II indicate an imbalance in that dosha. For example, if you are naturally Pitta-predominant (answered most questions as b) in Part I, but answered more questions as

Vata (a) in Part II, it suggests that you are experiencing a Vata imbalance.

Prakruti Results
a. Vata:

b. Pitta:

c. Kapha:

Vikruti Results
a. Vata:

b. Pitta:

c. Kapha:

Recommendations to balance each dosha

These recommendations are introductory and general. Each individual's needs are unique. Guidance from a qualified Ayurvedic practitioner can help you develop a personalized and detailed treatment plan to address specific imbalances and help promote optimal health and wellness.

Vata Dosha

Vata-predominant individuals tend to be thin, have a light frame, dry skin and hair, and tend to be restless, creative, and quick-thinking. When imbalanced, they may experience anxiety, insomnia, digestive issues, and joint pain.

To balance your Vata, try following a warm, nourishing diet with plenty of healthy fats and warm spices. A routine with adequate rest, relaxation, and self-care practices can also be beneficial. Warm oil massages, gentle yoga, and meditation can help soothe the nervous system and promote balance.

Pitta Dosha

Pitta-predominant individuals tend to be of medium build with good muscle tone, warm skin and hair, and tend to be driven, focused, and goal-oriented. When imbalanced, they may experience inflammation, digestive issues, anger, and frustration.

To balance your Pitta, try following a cooling, calming diet with plenty of fresh, whole foods and avoid spicy and oily foods. Regular exercise, especially during cooler times of day, can also help balance Pitta. Engaging in calming practices such as meditation, pranayama, and spending time in nature can also help soothe and balance Pitta.

Kapha Dosha

Kapha-predominant individuals tend to be of larger build, have soft, supple skin and hair, and tend to be grounded, nurturing, and patient. When imbalanced, they may experience weight gain, lethargy, respiratory issues, and depression.

To balance your Kapha, try following a light, warming diet with plenty of spices and vegetables. Regular exercise, especially vigorous activities like cardio, can help balance Kapha. Engaging in stimulating practices such as invigorating yoga, meditation, and socializing with friends and family can also help stimulate and balance Kapha.

Meditation
The Art of Observing Ourselves

The Journey Back to Silence

The art of observing ourselves requires more than merely a mirror. It requires us to be in and fully aware of the present moment. In every moment, we make a fundamental choice: to either be engaged with the present or to ignore it. The practice of meditation is one of the best ways to train yourself to be aware of the present.

When I went on my first meditation retreat many years ago, the teacher jokingly said that if you start meditating regularly, one of two things will happen: you'll either move to California or quit your job. While I didn't move to the West Coast, three years later I resigned from my full-time job to start my business as an independent consultant. I can't say that meditation was the only reason for my decision, but it was certainly a powerful and gentle force that helped me transform my life in a positive way.

Meditation empowers you to take charge of your inner narrative. With each moment of stillness and self-reflection, the protagonist within you grows stronger, more resilient, and more attuned to your limitless potential.

Observing yourself is an important element in becoming the protagonist of your own life. Meditation cultivates the ability to observe your thoughts, emotions, and sensations without getting caught up in or reacting to them. Practicing self-awareness allows you to gain insight into your mind and to develop a greater sense of clarity and calm.

How to Meditate

The Yoga Sutras are foundational texts of classical yoga, and they contain many teachings on the practice of meditation. The sage Patanjali wrote the Yoga Sutras around 2,000 years ago and chapter two is particularly relevant to meditation, as it outlines the practices that can lead to spiritual growth and self-realization. In this chapter, Patanjali describes the eight limbs of yoga, or Ashtanga, which include ethical guidelines, physical postures, breath control, and meditation.

The seventh limb of yoga is called Dhyana, the practice of meditation. According to the Yoga Sutras, meditation involves cultivating a single-pointed focus on a chosen object, such as the breath, a mantra, or an image. Through sustained practice, the mind becomes progressively more focused and still, leading to a state of deep concentration and inner peace.

Besides outlining the practice of meditation, the Yoga Sutras describe the many benefits of regular meditation practice. These include increased self-awareness, mental clarity, and spiritual growth, as well as a greater sense of connection to the divine and the world. The Yoga Sutras may have been written centuries ago, but it turns out the benefits of meditation are timeless. Just think of it as the original life hack for increased focus, no smartphone required.

When we meditate, we take the time to focus our attention on the present moment and to let go of our usual preoccupations and distractions. By doing so, we become more aware of the patterns and habits of our own mind, including our tendencies to judge, analyze, or react impulsively. Through regular practice, we develop the capacity to witness our own thoughts and feelings with greater detachment and equanimity, allowing us to recognize and let go of habitual patterns of thought and behavior that may cause us stress or suffering.

Among the many immense benefits meditation has provided me, the feeling of equanimity stands out as one of the greatest. Equanimity is a state of balance and calmness, a quality of mind that allows us to remain steady and composed in the face of life's challenges, without being swept away by intense emotions or thoughts. Equanimity enables us to observe our inner experiences, observing them with non-judgmental acceptance, so we can respond to whatever arises with clarity, wisdom, and compassion.

Over the past few years, I've experienced the impact of meditation more prominently, particularly in the face of a world pandemic, social unrest, and political upheaval. There was a time when simply watching the news would leave me distressed, and that feeling would linger and interfere with my daily activities and relationships for days. While I still have thoughts and feelings related to what's happening around me, I'm now able to acknowledge and accept them without getting caught up in them. This has allowed me to feel things deeply, but also let go and stay focused on the present moment. I'm now able to take conscious and intentional actions to benefit the world around me, without allowing these events to consume my entire life.

I have found meditation to be the easiest, hardest, simplest, and most difficult thing to practice. It is easy to learn, and it is free! It's simple because it doesn't require any special equipment, materials, or even a specific location. But it is hard because it requires carving out time, and it is difficult because it requires a great deal of discipline and consistency to develop a regular practice.

Although we understand the many benefits of meditation and how it can improve our lives, it can still be challenging to maintain a meditation routine. It is essential to remind ourselves continuously of the value of meditation and the positive impact it can have on our well-being. By practicing meditation more frequently, we can break out of unhealthy patterns and create newer, more effective ones.

It is also essential to acknowledge that life can be unpredictable, and we may not always be able to maintain our meditation practice. However, we should not judge ourselves but simply accept it is okay to fall off the wagon. Recommitting to the practice can happen any time. By cultivating a non-judgmental attitude toward ourselves, we can create a more sustainable and compassionate relationship with our meditation practice, making it easier to integrate it into our daily lives.

If you've been away from your meditation practice for a while, don't worry! You can always come back to it. Take a deep breath, pause what you're doing, and set aside a few minutes to meditate. You deserve this time to reconnect with yourself. Remember: meditation is a journey, and every step counts. So don't be unnecessarily hard on yourself. Embrace the present moment, and take that step toward your practice right now. You got this!

If you've never tried meditation before, don't let that stop you from experiencing the amazing benefits it can offer. You can start right now by making a choice to prioritize your mental and emotional wellbeing. Take a deep breath, clear your mind, and set aside just a few minutes to give it a try. You'll be surprised at how quickly you can feel a sense of calm and clarity. It's never too late to begin, and the benefits are waiting for you.

Meditation and Stress

Meditation is a powerful tool for understanding and managing stress. When you meditate, you cultivate an awareness of your thoughts, emotions, and physical sensations, allowing you to observe your experience with greater clarity and perspective. This awareness helps you to recognize the signs and symptoms of stress in your life and understand how they impact your mental, emotional, and physical well-being.

Through meditation, you can develop the ability to respond to stress in a more mindful and compassionate manner, rather than reacting impulsively. You learn to approach stressful situations with greater calmness and clarity, allowing you to make more conscious choices and avoid getting swept up in a cycle of negative thoughts and emotions.

As I write this paragraph, I am in a highly stressful situation. I live on the west coast of Florida, and Hurricane Ian is about to make landfall 30 miles south of where I live. This is literally happening in the next three hours. My family and I are outside the mandatory evacuation zones and we decided to stay home. We are expecting a category 4 or 5 hurricane. Today more than ever, I am thinking about all the tools I have to stay as calm and balanced as possible so I can continue to serve those around me.

Stress activates our sympathetic nervous system and flips us into a fight-or-flight response. Our bodies produce cortisol and adrenaline, our blood pressure increases, and we go on high alert. Recognizing when we are in this state can help us make choices to counterbalance the stress. How do we do this? I always start with deep breathing. As I write this, with a hurricane bearing down and my heart rate racing, I am reminding myself to take some deep breaths.

When we consciously breathe deeply, we activate our parasympathetic nervous system and the vagus nerve. This slows down our heart rate and lowers our blood pressure. It calms the body and mind. Deep breathing uses abdominal muscles and the diaphragm, which improves the efficiency of oxygen exchange and reduces strain on the muscles of the neck and upper chest. And I can really use some relaxation in my shoulder and neck muscles during this high-stress situation.

On a side note, Ayurvedically speaking, we are dealing with a huge Vata increase from Mother Nature's powerful winds. As we talked about in the previous chapter, Wind or Air is associated with the Vata dosha, which governs movement and communication in the body. When the Vata dosha is out of balance, it can cause disturbances in the body and mind, including anxiety, restlessness, and insomnia. Similarly, when the element of Air is imbalanced in nature, it can lead to violent storms and hurricanes.

The Vata increase is making everyone in our area feel out of balance: fearful, scared, and anxious. Knowing that "like increases like and opposites balance," I can seek opposite elements to balance the excess Air. I need grounding. I need Earth and the stability it brings.

Studies have shown that the Earth functions like a massive battery. To ensure safety and stability, almost everything in the electrical world is connected to it, including our refrigerators. This is what it means to be "grounded." By attaching a wire from the fridge's metal frame to the ground, any unwanted electricity is directed out of the wire and into the Earth. But here's the cool part: the concept of being grounded also applies to us humans. When we're electrically grounded, we feel centered, strong, balanced, and less stressed. It's like we become one with the Earth's energy, which helps us feel more connected to ourselves and the world.

So, as I'm writing this, I'm reminding myself that I need to get grounded. It's easy to get caught up in the chaos of daily life, but taking a moment to connect with the Earth's energy can help us feel more at ease, focused, and ready to take on whatever comes our way.

Many of us spend most of our time indoors, whether at work or in our homes. This means we're often cut off from the Earth's energy. We wear shoes with rubber soles that insulate us from electrical contact with the ground. We work and live in tall buildings, far removed from the natural world. As a result, we may feel ungrounded, tense, and stressed.

It's important to remember that we're part of a larger system that includes the Earth's subtle electrical charge. By connecting with this energy, we can feel more centered, solid, and balanced. Taking off our shoes and spending time outdoors can help us feel more grounded and in touch with the Earth.

Even if you're stuck indoors because of extreme weather, you can still ground yourself and connect with the Earth's energy. One of the quickest and simplest ways to do this is through breathwork and meditation.

The key is to find a grounding technique that works for you and make it a regular part of your routine. By doing so, you can stay connected to the Earth's energy and maintain a sense of balance and stability, even in difficult situations like a hurricane or other extreme events.

Thoughts

Prior to attending my first meditation retreat, I had a simplistic view of meditation as merely sitting in silence and attempting to stop thinking for a few minutes. I believed I didn't require a teacher to learn such a basic practice and that it didn't have to be done daily. It wasn't until I understood the true nature of meditation that I realized how it could drastically change my life.

Contrary to common misconceptions, meditation does not aim to eliminate thoughts from our minds. As Descartes famously stated in the 17th century, "I think, therefore I am."

Thinking is an essential part of our existence. So what exactly is meditation if it's not about getting rid of our thoughts?

Meditation is a journey back to inner silence. It is not a thing we do once and we are good. Meditation is actually not about *doing* at all. It is about *being*. When we meditate, we practice getting into quieter levels of the thinking process. At some point, we slip into a space between our thoughts: the space of infinite silence and possibilities, of pure awareness and pure potential. We slip into the infinite field of intelligence, and from that vantage point, we can observe ourselves.

Meditation is also an antidote to stress. Meditation allows us to remove layers of stress we have accumulated our entire lives, and with those layers removed, we are revealed. Then we can actually see who we really are.

Again, if you already have a meditation practice, then consider this a gentle reminder you are well on your way to becoming the protagonist of your life. And if you haven't yet started a meditation practice, now is an excellent moment to begin.

Hundreds, if not thousands, of meditation techniques exist because of the rich diversity of cultures and traditions throughout the world. This chapter's intention is not to cover all styles of meditation, but I do want to highlight three techniques I have found impactful in my life.

Breathing Meditation

My Ayurvedic mentor, Yashoda Ma, once referred to the breath as "our best friend." The breath was there for us the moment we were born and it will be with us until the very end of our lives. We are never alone. This idea has always given me such comfort. No matter where we go or what we do, our breath is always with us. It's a constant and reliable source of support that we can tap into whenever we need it.

We take about half a billion breaths between our first and our last. Our breathing is influenced by our thoughts, and our thoughts and physiology can be influenced by our breath. Awareness of the breath reduces stress immediately, helps us ground, clears and centers the mind, revitalizes the body, and improves physical well-being.

The breath can help us regulate our emotions. When we're feeling stressed or overwhelmed, our breathing often becomes shallow and rapid. By focusing on slowing down and deepening our breath, we can activate our parasympathetic nervous system, which helps us relax and feel calmer.

The breath can help us stay present. When we focus on our breath, we bring our attention to the present moment. This helps us let go of worries about the future or regrets about the past, and allows us to fully experience the richness of being here and now.

The breath can also improve our physical health. Deep breathing can lower our heart rate and blood pressure, reduce inflammation in the body, and improve lung function. It's also been shown to boost the immune system and enhance the body's natural healing processes.

Just like there are many meditation techniques, there are many breathing techniques, called Pranayama, which is a Sanskrit term that refers to the ancient practice of breath control in yoga. It is composed of two words: *prana*, which means life force or energy, and *yama*, which means control or restraint. Together, pranayama translates as the regulation of one's life force through breath control. Pranayama is the fourth of the Eight Limbs of Yoga, as described by the ancient sage Patanjali in the Yoga Sutras.

Pranayama techniques involve various breathing exercises and patterns designed to enhance physical and mental well-being. These practices include alternate nostril breathing, deep breathing, breath retention, and more. Pranayama is often incorporated into yoga classes to prepare the body and mind for meditation, and can also be practiced on its own as a standalone practice.

Alternate Nostril Breathing

Alternate nostril breathing, also known as Nadi Shodhana, is a Pranayama technique that involves breathing through alternate nostrils. It is a simple and effective way to balance the flow of prana in the body, calm the mind, and reduce stress and anxiety. Here's how to practice alternate nostril breathing. I encourage you to try it as you read this:

1. Sit comfortably with your spine straight and your shoulders relaxed.

2. Bring your right hand up to your face and use your right thumb to close your right nostril.

3. Inhale through your left nostril for a count of 4.

4. Use your right ring finger to close your left nostril and hold your breath for a count of 4.

5. Release your right thumb and exhale through your right nostril for a count of 4.

6. Inhale through your right nostril for a count of 4.

7. Use your right thumb to close your right nostril and hold your breath for a count of 4.

8. Release your ring finger and exhale through your left nostril for a count of 4.

9. This completes one round. Repeat for several rounds, gradually increasing the count of the breaths to 6, 8, or more.

You can practice alternate nostril breathing any time of day, but is especially useful as a prelude to other kinds of meditation or when you need to calm your mind and reduce stress. It's important to breathe deeply and evenly, without forcing the breath, and to keep your attention focused on your breath throughout the practice.

Deep Breathing

Deep breathing, also known as diaphragmatic breathing or belly breathing, is a technique that involves breathing deeply into the belly rather than shallowly into the chest. It is a simple and effective way to reduce stress, calm the mind and body, and increase feelings of relaxation and well-being.

Here's how to practice deep breathing. Again, let's do it together:

1. Find a comfortable seated or lying position, with your spine straight and your shoulders relaxed.

2. Place your hands on your belly, and take a slow, deep breath in through your nose, allowing your belly to expand as you inhale.

3. Hold the breath for a moment, and then exhale slowly and completely through your mouth, feeling your belly fall back towards your spine.

4. Repeat this pattern of inhaling deeply into your belly and exhaling slowly through your mouth for several rounds, focusing on the sensation of your breath and the movement of your belly.

As you practice deep breathing, it's helpful to count the length of your inhale and exhale, gradually lengthening each over time. For example, you might inhale for a count of four, hold for a count of two, and exhale for a count of six. Counting helps to focus your attention on the breath and bring your awareness to the present moment. It gives you something concrete to focus on, preventing your mind from wandering and helping to cultivate mindfulness.

Deep breathing, particularly with a longer exhale, activates the parasympathetic nervous system, which promotes relaxation and counters the effects of stress and anxiety.

It's important to breathe deeply and evenly, without forcing the breath, and to keep your attention focused on your breath throughout the practice. With regular practice, deep breathing can become a natural and automatic way of breathing, helping you to feel more calm and centered in your daily life.

Breath Retention

Breath retention, also known as Kumbhaka, is a pranayama technique that involves holding the breath after inhaling or exhaling. It is an advanced technique that should be practiced under the guidance of a qualified teacher, as it can have powerful effects on the body and mind.

Here's how to practice breath retention:

1. Sit comfortably with your spine straight and your shoulders relaxed.

2. Take a slow, deep breath in through your nose, filling your lungs completely.

3. Hold your breath for a count of 2 to 4, or for as long as feels comfortable.

4. Exhale slowly and completely through your nose, emptying your lungs completely.

5. Hold your breath after exhaling for a count of 2 to 4, or for as long as feels comfortable.

6. Inhale deeply again and repeat the cycle for several rounds.

It's important to start slowly and gradually increase the time you hold your breath, as holding your breath for too long can be stressful on the body and can lead to dizziness or lightheadedness. It's also important to listen to your body and not push yourself beyond your limits.

Breath retention can have a variety of benefits, including improving lung capacity, increasing energy, reducing stress, and promoting a deeper sense of relaxation and concentration. However, it should be practiced with caution, and should not be practiced by people with certain medical conditions, such as high blood pressure, heart disease, or respiratory problems. It's always best to consult with a qualified teacher or healthcare provider before beginning any new pranayama practice.

Remember, anytime you are feeling stressed, whether you are dealing with a hurricane or simply running late for work, you can use your breath to shift your state of being. Just close your lips and breathe through your nose. Trace the movement of your inhale and exhale and focus on long exhalations. Relax your jaw. Let your tongue fall away from the roof of your mouth. Unclench any clenched teeth. Repeat for as long as you need until you feel centered.

Mantra Meditation

During my teacher training at the Chopra Meditation Program, I was reminded that we are not "human *doings*," but "human *beings*." This concept emphasizes the importance of being aware in the present moment, rather than always striving to achieve more and do more. It suggests that our value and worth as individuals are not solely determined by what we accomplish, but by our inherent nature as human beings.

Measuring our self-worth based on our accomplishments, productivity, and success can lead to a sense of pressure, stress, and anxiety as we strive to do more in order to feel validated and accepted by others.

However, the idea of being a "human being" suggests there is inherent value simply in existing, without the constant need to achieve or accomplish something. Of course, this does not mean we should not strive to improve ourselves or pursue our goals and dreams. Rather, it means that we should approach these pursuits from a place of inner peace and contentment, rather than from a place of anxiety or pressure.

For so many of us, myself included, who feel like they should be "doing" something most of the time, Mantra meditation can be extremely helpful. Mantra meditation involves repeating a word, phrase, or sound (known as a mantra) to help focus the mind and achieve a deep state of relaxation and concentration. Repeating a mantra gives you something to "do" and it is a powerful tool for quieting the mind, reducing stress and anxiety, and increasing feelings of peace and wellbeing.

This is one of my favorite styles of meditation and the one I practice the most. Another concept I learned in my meditation teacher training is that everything in creation is a sound or vibration. The Big OM that started the Universe is still happening through constant vibration. Every rock, person, object, plant, and animal has its own unique vibration. The emotions we feel, the qualities we express in life, and every single thought... all are vibrations.

The idea that everything is vibration is a fundamental concept in many spiritual and scientific traditions. In physics, the concept of vibration is related to the field of quantum mechanics, which studies the behavior of particles at the atomic and subatomic level. According to this perspective, all matter is composed of tiny particles that are constantly in motion, vibrating at different frequencies to create the various forms and structures we observe in the physical world.

In spiritual and metaphysical traditions, the concept of vibration is often associated with the idea that everything has an energetic frequency that can influence our thoughts, emotions, and experiences. For example, the vibrations of certain colors, sounds, and words have specific effects on the mind and body, and can be used for healing, meditation, and other spiritual practices.

The idea that everything vibrates suggests there is an underlying interconnectedness and unity to the universe, and that we are all connected to each other and to the larger cosmic fabric of existence. By cultivating an awareness of the vibrational nature of reality, we can see the world in a more holistic and interconnected way, and develop a greater sense of harmony and balance in our lives.

Many cultures and traditions around the world use sounds and vibrations to heal, to celebrate, and to transform. Drums, bells, gongs, chants, and sounds of nature all have a unique effect on our mind-bodies.

Our mind is filled with sounds and words that carry a unique vibratory pattern, which changes with the natural flow of our thoughts. Every word we think or say has a particular effect in our lives. When we can control our inner speech, we can control our minds.

If meditation is a journey, then mantras are the means of transport. Mantras are the vehicle that carry us from our outer world to our inner world, back to silence. Mantra is often translated from Sanskrit as "vehicle of the mind." Mantra meditation connects us to the greater cosmic sounds of the universe, linking our outer speech with our inner speech.

Our thoughts have not only a sound and a vibration, they also have a meaning. The meaning from whatever thought or word is in our minds leads us to another thought, which leads us to another thought and so forth. Our minds are always in an active state.

Mantras don't always have a literal meaning. Mantras can just be sounds. According to the Vedic tradition, the ancient sages in India could hear the subtle vibrations and sounds produced by everything in nature: wind, rain, thunder, birds and butterflies, rivers and oceans. They recognized these sounds as the manifestation of spirit into matter and recorded them in Vedic literature using Sanskrit.

When we use sound-based, non-literal mantras in meditation, we help our mind get out of the active level. The more we bring our attention to the repetition of a mantra, the easier it is to settle the mind into a deeper, calmer level.

When the sages in India recorded mantras, they recognized 108 different vibrations that repeat with every lunar cycle. We call these vibrations Primordial Sound Mantras.

Primordial Sound Meditation (PSM) is based on these mantras and is the signature method of the Chopra Meditation Program. A qualified and certified teacher can calculate which of these mantras was vibrating at the moment of someone's birth. Through Vedic mathematics and the knowledge of the date, time, and location of your birth, you can discover your own unique vibration and use it in meditation. When you meditate with your own mantra, you not only reconnect with your most fundamental level of being, but you also allow your mind to experience deeper levels of awareness. As a practitioner and certified teacher of PSM, I can attest this is an effective tool for managing stress and improving overall well-being.

Until you have a Primordial Sound Mantra calculated for you by a certified teacher, there is a universal mantra that can be used by anyone: "So Hum." Although we don't want to focus on literal meaning, the mantra "So Hum" represents the unity and interconnectedness of all things. It is a reminder that we are all part of a larger whole and that our true nature is not separate from the surrounding universe. By meditating on this mantra, we can cultivate a sense of connection and harmony with the world.

Here are the steps to practice "So Hum" meditation:

1. Find a quiet and comfortable place where you can sit undisturbed for at least 10-15 minutes.

2. Sit in a comfortable position, either on a cushion or a chair with your back straight, and close your eyes.

3. Take a few deep breaths, inhaling through your nose and exhaling through your mouth, to relax your body and mind.

4. Repeat the mantra "So Hum" silently to yourself on your inhale and exhale. As you inhale, silently say "So" to yourself, and as you exhale, silently say "Hum" to yourself. Mentally repeat or think the word without actually vocalizing it out loud. You do not need to move your lips or mouth. Instead, you focus on the internal repetition of the word within your mind.

5. Focus your attention on the sound of the mantra as you repeat it, allowing your breath and the sound of the mantra to become one.

6. If your mind wanders or you become distracted, gently bring your attention back to the sound of the mantra and your breath.

7. Continue to repeat the mantra for at least 10-15 minutes, or as long as it feels comfortable for you.

8. When you are ready to end your practice, slowly bring your attention back to your breath, and take a few deep breaths before opening your eyes.

You can practice mantra meditation any time of day, but it can be especially helpful as a daily practice first thing in the morning and before bed. It's important to approach mantra meditation with a spirit of openness and curiosity, allowing the practice to unfold naturally and without judgment. If you practice with respect and patience, mantra meditation can be a deeply transformative practice, helping you to connect with your inner self and find greater peace and clarity in your daily life.

Be sure to seek the guidance of a qualified teacher if you have questions.

Mindfulness Meditation

Mindfulness is the practice of being fully present and engaged in the current moment, without judgment or distraction. It involves paying attention to our thoughts, feelings, and physical sensations with curiosity and openness, and developing an awareness of our habitual patterns and reactions.

When we practice mindfulness, we become more attuned to our own needs and desires, as well as the needs and desires of those around us. This can help us become more effective communicators and collaborators, and can also help us develop deeper and more meaningful relationships.

Becoming the protagonist of our own lives means taking an active role in shaping our experiences and pursuing our goals and desires. It means being intentional about how we spend our time and energy, and being willing to take risks and make changes in order to create the life we truly want.

The practice of mindfulness can help us become more aware of our own wants and needs, as well as how we may be holding ourselves back or sabotaging our own progress. By developing a greater sense of self-awareness and self-compassion, we can make more conscious choices about how we want to show up in the world and what we want to create for ourselves.

Rooted in the Buddhist tradition, mindfulness is an ongoing life practice that addresses what is going on in the moment and works to release it right away. Mindfulness meditation includes a wide range of practices, such as mindful eating, walking, observing the world, driving, doing the dishes, breathing, or sitting in stillness.

One of my favorite mindfulness practices uses the acronym STOP. Each letter in the word STOP represents a specific step in the practice:

S - STOP: When you notice you are feeling stressed, anxious, or overwhelmed, pause whatever you are doing and allow yourself to step away from the situation. Simply give yourself a moment of space.

T - TAKE A BREATH: Take a few slow, deep breaths, focusing on the sensation of the breath moving in and out of your body. Allow yourself to release any tension or discomfort as you exhale.

O - OBSERVE: Observe your thoughts and emotions without judgment. Notice what thoughts or feelings are present, and where in your body you are experiencing them. Just observe them without trying to change them or push them away.

P - PROCEED: After you have taken a moment to pause, breathe, and observe, consider your options. Ask yourself which action would be most helpful and aligned with your goals and values. Then make a conscious decision to proceed.

The STOP practice is a simple but powerful tool for developing mindfulness and self-awareness. You can use it in a variety of situations, from managing stress to responding effectively to difficult situations or interactions. By taking a pause, focusing on our breath, and observing our thoughts and emotions, we can become more present, grounded, and clear-headed, which then enables us to make more skillful choices in our lives.

Whatever form of meditation you decide to try, it is important to practice it for at least a month to see its changes and benefits. Meditation is not about getting it *right*. It is about *practice*. And repetition is key in any practice. Thoughts will be there. They are a part of the practice, and it is important to accept them and let them go. We should not hold on to any expectation regarding the practice. Less is more.

Side Benefits

You may have heard the phrase that meditation has no side effects, just side benefits. Meditation has many tangible benefits for mental and physical health besides dealing with a hurricane. Countless research and books cover the science behind all these benefits, ranging from improving the brain, focus, memory, creativity, and problem solving to decreasing depression, anxiety, and insomnia.

The more we meditate, the more aware we become. We can notice when we are off balance. We can become mindful of our feelings and thoughts. And we can make conscious choices every moment.

Marcel Proust wrote, "The real journey of discovery is not in seeking new landscapes, but in seeing with new eyes." In our hero's journey to become our life's protagonist, meditation enables us to observe our lives and surroundings from a new perspective.

Meditation Tips

Despite the ancient knowledge and modern research confirming the benefits of meditation, it has yet to become a mainstream practice. While some may try then give up, others never attempt it at all. However, I believe that understanding the practicalities of meditation could benefit everyone, whether or not they currently meditate. So I will outline some helpful tips related to meditation.

When preparing to meditate, a fancy pillow or specific yoga position is unnecessary. All you need is a comfortable and safe place to sit and close your eyes, which could be your living room, car, airport, train, or work desk during lunchtime.

It is preferable to close your eyes when meditating unless you are practicing mindful meditation techniques such as walking, in order to minimize distractions and focus inward. You should aim to practice meditation daily, ideally twice a day, before and after your busiest daily activities. Start with a few minutes and gradually increase the practice's duration.

When you finally sit down and close your eyes to meditate, you may experience various images, pictures, or sensations in your mind and body. However, treat them the same way you handle thoughts during the practice: simply notice them, let them go, and gently return your attention to the meditation.

You should not judge the success of your meditation by the experiences you have during the practice. Instead, you can assess its effectiveness by asking yourself if you feel more relaxed and happier, more balanced and intuitive, and less stressed. Regular meditation can provide these benefits, which will grow over time.

By practicing meditation regularly, you can increase your awareness, balance, and intuition, which can lead to greater clarity and purpose in your life. So, whether you are a seasoned meditator or new to the practice, remember that meditation can help you become the hero of your own story and live a more fulfilling and meaningful life.

Theater
The Art of Observing Human Actions

The Roles We Play in Life

Although music was my first love, it was the discovery of theater that truly transformed me. I moved to the United States to pursue Musical Theater, but with a strong musical background, I knew I needed to immerse myself in the theatrical side of my conservatory program.

As I started auditioning, I faced the harsh reality of typecasting. As a Brazilian immigrant, my accent limited my ability to play traditional American roles. Directors considered me too white for many Latinx parts, and simultaneously often asked me to adopt various European accents to play French, German, Russian, or other white European characters. Through this experience, I gained a profound insight into the complexities of human actions and the impact of representation in the performing arts.

As an immigrant, one inevitably takes on the role of an observer. Even if you can learn the language quickly, everything else in the culture is different, new, and unfamiliar. Comprehending the norms and expectations of a new environment requires observation and learning. The language I gained during my theater training enhanced my experience as an observer-immigrant.

Actors are adept at playing different roles. We are attuned to the nuances of verbal and nonverbal communication and skilled in observing life to portray it on stage. As I delved deeper into the craft of acting, I recognized parallels between my performances on stage and my life offstage.

Early in my career, I played the captivating character of Lady Nijo in the thought-provoking play *Top Girls*. Written by Caryl Churchill, the play delves into the struggles and triumphs of women from different historical periods, weaving their stories together in a powerful exploration of feminism, ambition, and identity. Lady Nijo, one of the pivotal historical figures, is a 13th-century Japanese imperial concubine who embarks on a transformative journey from a life of privilege and restriction to one of spiritual enlightenment and self-discovery.

Her courage to break free from societal norms and find her voice reminded me of the importance of embracing authenticity and staying true to one's inner calling, no matter how unconventional it may seem. As I delved into the depths of her character, I uncovered my own inner strength and embraced my unique journey.

Her tenacity in navigating a world dominated by patriarchy taught me the significance of advocating for oneself and embracing personal power. Witnessing her unyielding determination to forge her own path, I recognized the necessity of standing up for what I believe in and using my voice to make a difference in the world.

Through my portrayal of Lady Nijo, I embarked on a personal journey of self-discovery and self-acceptance. I learned to embrace the complexity of my identity, recognizing that every facet of who I am contributes to my growth. Her story served as a powerful reminder that embracing all aspects of ourselves, even the ones that may seem challenging or unconventional, is crucial in our pursuit of self-discovery.

As I mentioned above, there are complex issues of identity when it comes to casting in the theater. As a Brazilian immigrant who presents white, portraying a character like Lady Nijo—who is Japanese—raised important questions about the evolving standards of appropriateness in casting. This experience made me question not only how I was cast, but also how I perceived myself in a world where cultural backgrounds and appearances can often define our roles.

This had happened back in Brazil, too. I vividly remember being cast in roles for musical theater that were not typecast. For example, I played Puerto Rican and Asian characters. As long as I could sing the part, it didn't matter what I looked like.

This contrast in casting practices between countries under-scored the fluidity and diversity of theatrical representation.

Best practices in casting continue to evolve, as they should, to account for the lack of representation in the past. But I've also realized that the concept of *presentation* in the theater world has striking parallels to the way people navigate their lives offstage. The labels and categories assigned to us in cast-ing can mirror the societal roles we inhabit in our daily exis-tence. Theater serves as a microcosm for broader societal dis-cussions on identity, representation, and individual agency.

In an ever-evolving world where authenticity and individu-ality are increasingly celebrated, casting choices and audience perceptions reflect the ongoing journey toward self-discov-ery and self-acceptance. These considerations go beyond the stage, as they raise essential questions about how each of us becomes the protagonist of our own life narrative, regardless of the roles and labels society may assign us.

Doing the work of digging into characters—and discov-ering myself inside them—led me to rediscover the works of Brazilian theater director, writer, and political activist Augus-to Boal.

I initially encountered Augusto Boal through his work as a lyricist for some of my favorite songs when I was growing up in Brazil. Once I became an immigrant, I gained a more profound appreciation for Boal's legacy and the incredible contributions he made to the world through the Theater of the Oppressed movement.

At first, I was confused and regretful. How could it be that teachers did not expose me to such an important figure in my culture during my education in Brazil? Why did I have to move to a different country to learn about his groundbreaking work? While excluded from the knowledge of my own cultural heritage, I was also filled with a newfound sense of pride as a Brazilian, which was not something I had experienced much while growing up.

That is when I decided I needed to learn more about Boal and his work. Coupled with my personal experience as an immigrant actor, I felt a sense of responsibility to effect positive change through the arts. As a result, I pursued a Master's degree in Intercultural Relations with a focus on Arts for Social Change.

For those who are not familiar, the Theater of the Oppressed is a form of popular education and social activism that was developed by Augusto Boal in the 1960s. It is a technique that aims to empower marginalized communities and promote social justice by using theater as a means of political expression and social change.

The basic idea of the Theater of the Oppressed is to create a space where individuals can express their experiences of oppression, and then explore ways to resist and overcome it. This approach to theater aims to create a dialogue that is democratic, participatory, and transformative.

One of Boal's key contributions in Theater of the Oppressed was the development of Forum Theater, which is a form of applied theater that explores different scenarios related to a specific issue or problem. In Forum Theater, a play is performed, and then the audience is invited to participate by suggesting alternative endings or solutions to the problem presented in the play. Through this process, both actors and audience members can explore different perspectives, practice assertiveness and communication, and gain a greater sense of agency and control over their lives.

I was living in the United States for 4 years when I found myself in my first Forum Theater workshop with Augusto Boal. To my surprise, I was chosen to play the antagonist—the character perceived as a source of conflict and oppression who was the mother of the protagonist. Nervous yet determined, I delved into her mindset, discovering the intricacies that shaped her actions.

As I embodied the antagonist, I realized she was more than a two-dimensional villain; she was human, with vulnerabilities, fears and her own internal oppressions. This experience taught me the power of empathy and compassion for characters whose actions may seem difficult to understand.

Beyond the stage, the workshop shed light on a broader truth: sometimes, we unknowingly become antagonists in other people's lives. This newfound awareness fueled my commitment to approach others with empathy and understanding, acknowledging that everyone has their unique struggles and complexities.

The interactive nature of the workshop amplified its impact, showcasing how collective dialogue can transform narratives of conflict. This transformative experience strengthened my belief in theater's ability to foster connections, break down barriers, and promote a more inclusive and empathetic society.

Stepping into the antagonist's shoes became a defining moment, inspiring me to navigate both my artistic journey and life with empathy, openness, and a commitment to making a positive impact. It reminded me that, in understanding others, we foster a more compassionate world.

Boal believed theater could be a powerful tool for social change, and that people who created and performed theater could become active agents of change in their own lives and communities. Through his work, Boal created a range of exercises that could create interactive and participatory theater experiences that could challenge oppression and promote social justice.

Boal also developed the concept of "spect-actor," meaning someone can be both the spectator and the actor in the theater. He believed we could be spect-actors not just on stage but also in real life. Being both observer and participant aligns with being the protagonist of your own life and shaping your own destiny.

While all forms of art offer unique and powerful ways of understanding and experiencing the world, in my opinion, theater stands out as the art form that everyone should learn. Echoing the words of Augusto Boal, theater is significant because it organizes human actions in both space and time, offering a profound insight into our past, present, and future. Theater helps us gain a better understanding of ourselves, our emotions, and our aspirations. Essentially, theater is the art of observing and understanding human actions.

Theater as a Martial Art

The concept of "Theater as a Martial Art" was also developed by Augusto Boal. Boal's work in theater was heavily influenced by his experiences as an activist in Brazil, where he was involved in the fight against the military dictatorship in the 1960s and 1970s.

According to Boal, just as martial arts involve a disciplined and rigorous training of the body and mind, so too does theater require a similar level of discipline and focus. In particular, Boal believed actors needed to develop a strong sense of awareness, both of their own bodies and of the surrounding space. This awareness would allow them to move with grace and precision on stage, while also remaining attuned to the needs and reactions of their fellow actors.

Theater can also cultivate a sense of empathy and compassion, which are central tenets of many martial arts. Through their performances, actors could explore the experiences and perspectives of others, and in doing so, develop a deeper understanding of the world around them. Creating powerful works of art helps to create a more just and equitable society.

Playing Many Roles

Our identities are complex and multifaceted. The idea that we play many roles in life relates not only to theater but also to the fields of psychology and sociology. This idea suggests that while we may assume various roles and identities throughout our lives, these roles do not define who we are at our core.

How we view ourselves varies based on our experiences, perceptions, and beliefs. Many factors can influence our view of ourselves, including our upbringing, cultural background, and social interactions.

Psychologists often describe the way we view ourselves as our "self-concept." Our self-concept includes our beliefs about our abilities, values, and personality traits. Our experiences and the feedback we receive from others shape it.

Our self-concept can also be influenced by the social roles we occupy. For example, we may view ourselves differently as a parent, friend, or employee. These different roles may emphasize different aspects of our personality and may affect our self-concept in different ways. While these roles may be important for our interactions with others, they do not reflect our truest self or our innermost desires and motivations.

Overall, our self-concept is a complex and dynamic construct that changes over time. It is shaped by a variety of internal and external factors and plays a significant role in how we perceive ourselves and interact with the world.

From a young age, we are socialized to conform to the expectations and norms of our culture. We learn these norms through our families, peers, schools, and media. This socialization shapes our behavior and beliefs, and we often internalize these norms and expectations as part of our identity. Becoming an immigrant caused a clash in my identity, as I had to navigate and adapt to different cultural expectations and norms.

Being Brazilian means I come from a collectivist culture. In a collectivist culture, the emphasis is on the group or community rather than the individual. People in collectivist cultures prioritize the needs and goals of the group over their own individual needs and desires. They may place a high value on conformity, interdependence, and harmony within the group.

An individualistic culture, however, such as the United States, emphasizes the individual rather than the group. People in individualistic cultures prioritize their own needs, goals, and desires over those of the group. They may place a high value on personal achievement, independence, and self-expression.

I completed most of my formal education in Brazil before pursuing my Master's degree in the United States. It was my first time in a formal education setting in the US, and one day a professor approached me about my lack of participation in class compared to my peers. Her observation surprised me, as I had been actively listening and following the discussions. However, in my collectivist cultural upbringing, I was taught to prioritize the needs of the group and to never interrupt a speaker. As a result, I often stayed quiet in class, especially when my classmates were already actively engaging in discussion. This experience highlighted the social norms of formal education in the US I was not accustomed to, and I felt pressured to go against my own cultural norms to comply with these expectations. It was a challenging change for me, and I still find it difficult to interrupt others in a discussion.

Social norms and expectations can create pressure to conform to the behaviors and attitudes that are acceptable within a particular culture or social group. This pressure to conform can influence our behavior, choices, and even our identity. We may feel that we need to meet certain expectations in order to be accepted or valued by others. To become the protagonist of our lives, we need to be aware of these influences and consider how they may be affecting our sense of self and our interactions with others.

Theater has given me a greater awareness of cultural nuances, and I now feel more at ease playing different roles in life. Although I am still mindful of the collective, I have grown more confident in individualistic settings. I have learned to mix cultural norms and identify opportunities to share my knowledge while navigating cultural differences. Today, I feel more comfortable blending these cultural perspectives in my life, and my theater training and performances gave me the tools to do so.

In theater, the concept of playing different roles is central to the art form. Actors must be able to embody different characters, often with very different personalities, motivations, and behaviors. One way to explore this theme is through the use of masks. Masks have been used in theater for thousands of years to represent different characters and emotions. By putting on a mask, actors can assume a different identity and explore different aspects of themselves and the human experience. The mask allows the actor to step out of their own identity and into the identity of the character they are portraying.

In addition to masks, other theatrical techniques explore the idea of playing different roles. For example, actors may use improvisation to explore different characters and scenarios, or they may work with a director to develop a character through script analysis and character development exercises.

Through these techniques, actors can highlight the idea that while we are able to assume many identities, these identities do not define us. By exploring different characters and roles, actors and audiences alike can gain a deeper understanding of the complexity of the human experience and the different identities we can inhabit.

Right after giving birth to my first child, Olivia, I was cast as "Lorna" in *Mammals* by English playwright Amelia Bullmore. I was simultaneously learning a new role for the play and a new role in life. Portraying the character of Lorna in *Mammals* became an unforgettable and deeply meaningful experience, especially because of my role as a new mom. Lorna's character resonated with me on a profound level as she explored the complexities of relationships, personal choices, and self-discovery.

Like Lorna, I found myself navigating a newfound vulnerability as a new mom, experiencing a mix of overwhelming emotions and a profound sense of responsibility for my newborn. The emotional journey of both Lorna and my role as a new mom enabled me to explore a range of feelings, from strength and determination to moments of doubt and uncertainty.

The aspect of balancing responsibilities was a shared theme between the two roles. As Lorna juggled her relationships and life choices, I, too, was learning to balance caring for my newborn, household tasks, and self-care. Through Lorna's experiences, I discovered parallels with the challenges of motherhood and how prioritizing one's time and energy is essential in both scenarios.

However, the most striking contrast between playing Lorna and being a new mom was the concept of independence versus dependency. As Lorna sought personal freedom and made choices to challenge norms, I found myself fully dedicated to nurturing and caring for my dependent newborn. Yet, through this contrast, I gained a deeper appreciation for the choices and sacrifices that come with motherhood and the strength that arises from selfless love.

Theater, in its transformative capacity, has helped me understand my new role as a mom by providing a unique platform to explore and express the complexities of human emotions and relationships. By embodying Lorna's character on stage, I tapped into a deeper understanding of vulnerability, resilience, and the multifaceted nature of being a woman. The exploration of similarities and contrasts between Lorna's journey and my role as a new mom allowed me to reflect on the universal aspects of the human experience, fostering empathy and compassion both in my acting and in my real-life interactions as a mother.

You can embrace the benefits of acting classes today, even without aspiring to be a professional actor. It's never too late to embark on a journey of learning and self-discovery. You can also experience the transformative power of theater by engaging in solo exercises from the comfort of your own home.

Here is an exercise you can do on your own to provide insights into the roles you play in life. [1]

1. Take a few minutes to sit quietly and reflect on the different voices inside of you. Imagine each voice as a distinct character, with its own personality and motivations.

2. Give each of these characters a name and write those names down on a piece of paper. Identify and choose three definitions of yourself, like teacher, writer, and mother, for example.

---

1. To download a free PDF copy of this exercise, visit http s://atomica-arts.com/the-roles-we-play-in-life/

3. Take a few minutes to think about each role, each character's wants, needs, and opinions. Write a brief description of each character's personality and motivations.

4. Once you clearly understand each character, imagine them having a conversation with one another. What would they say to each other? How would they interact?

5. After the conversation is over, take a few moments to reflect on what you have learned about yourself. Did any of the characters surprise you? Did you discover anything new about your wants, needs, or opinions?

Theater of the Oppressed and Playing Roles in Life

Through my work in Theater of the Oppressed, I have become a spect-actor many times. This process of being both performer and observer has also helped me understand the roles I play in life. I have developed a critical awareness of the social roles and expectations that we encounter in our lives. I have been able to observe how different characters on stage interact with one another and analyze the power dynamics at play. Understanding the power structures in my life and becoming more conscious of my roles and behaviors has been a transformative result of my work using Boal's techniques.

Applying theater to our lives and becoming a spect-actor can help us explore alternative possibilities for our own roles and behaviors. By observing the actions and choices of characters on stage, we can imagine different ways of responding to situations in our own lives. This can help us expand our sense of what is possible and challenge the constraints of the roles we play every single day.

Through spect-actor participation, we can also develop a deeper sense of empathy and connection with others. By stepping into the shoes of a character on stage and understanding their experiences and perspectives, we can develop greater compassion and understanding for the people in our lives and break down the barriers that separate us from others.

My experiences as a spect-actor have also provided me with a profound understanding of both my oppressions and my privileges. I have become acutely aware of when I hold power and when I don't, and this has transformed my relationships.

As a white Latina married to a Mexican man who has a very native appearance, we both navigate our social interactions through the lenses of our gender and race. Depending on the context, he may hold more power than me for being a man, especially when around other men. Conversely, in many situations, I may hold more power than him due to my whiteness. We each face our own forms of oppression, and we are both able to recognize and acknowledge each other's struggles. This heightened awareness has enabled us to support each other more effectively as we navigate the complexities of social interactions in the world.

I also realized that while I am the main character in my life story, I can also be the antagonist in someone else's narrative, depending on the power dynamic of the role I am playing. For example, as a parent, I hold more power than my daughters, who are the protagonists of their own lives. When I interfere with their wants or needs, such as by forbidding them from using their phones until they finish their homework, I take on the role of the antagonist in their story.

Becoming aware of the roles we play in life allows us to understand the impact we have on others. When we recognize the power dynamics of our roles, we can better appreciate the perspectives of those around us and empathize with their experiences. By understanding that we can be the protagonists or antagonists in someone else's story, we can strive to be more considerate and compassionate in our interactions with others. Ultimately, this awareness can help us build stronger relationships and lead more fulfilling lives.

The main theme of this book is to transform our lives by becoming the main character of our own story. However, the emphasis is on becoming a protagonist who is conscious and accountable for the well-being of our society as a whole. It's not just about personal success, but about contributing to the greater good and making the world a better place for everyone.

This is why I gravitate so strongly toward Theater of the Oppressed. The main goal of these techniques is to create a space for collective reflection and action. Theater of the Oppressed has been used around the world to tackle a range of issues, including gender inequality, racism, poverty, environmental degradation, and political oppression. Through the creation of theater pieces, workshops, and community-based projects, Theater of the Oppressed can empower communities to take action, challenge social norms and structures, and work towards a more just and equitable society.

Theater as Yoga

Theater has always been my Yoga. In Chapter 2, I referred to Yoga as the return of our body-mind to the infinite field of intelligence or pure consciousness. Theater, in its essence, serves as a transformative practice that allows us to reconnect with the infinite field of human emotions and collective consciousness, much like Yoga guides us to return our body-mind to the realm of pure consciousness.

Prior to practicing Yoga, I found theater served as my means of connecting breath and movement. Theater and Yoga are two practices that lead to self-discovery and personal growth. Both are ways to connect with one's inner self and to explore different aspects of one's being.

Theater and Yoga share similarities in the use of breath and movement. Both practices emphasize breath as a tool to connect the body to the mind and access deeper emotions and thoughts. Similarly, movement is utilized in both practices to physically express emotions and thoughts, further connecting the body and mind.

Additionally, both Theater and Yoga create connections with others and build community. Theater tells stories to explore shared experiences, building empathy and understanding. Likewise, Yoga builds a sense of community and connection through shared intentions and partner and group poses.

The ultimate aim of both is to cultivate self-awareness. By participating in these practices, we develop a deeper understanding of ourselves and the world. We step out of our usual roles and identities and explore different aspects of ourselves and the human experience. We cultivate a greater awareness of our bodies, emotions, and thoughts, and develop a more profound sense of connection to ourselves and others.

One exercise that connects both practices is called "The Mirror Exercise."

Here's how to do it:

1. Find a partner and stand facing each other. Make sure you have enough space to move freely.

2. Decide who will be the leader and who will be the follower for the first round. The leader will initiate movements and the follower will mirror them.

3. The leader will start by making a simple movement, such as raising their right arm. The follower should mirror this movement exactly, raising their left arm.

4. Continue with different movements, with the leader initiating and the follower mirroring. You can start with simple movements and gradually build up to more complex actions.

5. As you continue, try to stay connected with your partner and maintain eye contact. Pay attention to the details of each other's movements and try to mirror them as accurately as possible.

6. After a few minutes, switch roles and let the other person be the leader.

The goal of the exercise is to develop physical and emotional awareness, as well as a deeper connection with the partner. Through "The Mirror Exercise," participants engage in a nonverbal form of communication, relying on their observation and imitation skills to mirror each other's movements and postures. By staying connected and maintaining mindful awareness, the participants develop a heightened sense of empathy as they intuitively respond to their partner's actions.

The Role of the Imagination

The imagination is a potent tool for actors, allowing them to fully embody their characters and bring them to life on stage. By accessing different emotions, experiences, and perspectives, actors can enhance the authenticity of their performances and connect more deeply with their characters and the story they are telling.

However, developing a strong imagination is not just important for actors but for anyone seeking to become a more effective protagonist in their own lives. The imagination allows us to envision new possibilities, explore different perspectives, and tap into our creativity and intuition. By exercising our imagination, we can develop greater empathy and understanding for others, cultivate our unique perspectives, and discover new ways of approaching challenges and opportunities.

One of the key aspects of imagination is the ability to desire something different for ourselves and the world. When we desire something, we create an energetic pull towards that goal, and our imagination helps us to envision what that goal would look like if we were to achieve it. This helps us to focus our energy and attention on the steps we need to take to make that desire a reality.

Imagination also allows us to tap into our creativity and find new ways of approaching challenges and opportunities. When we use our imagination, we can see beyond the limitations of our current circumstances and envision new ways of being and doing. This can help us break free from old patterns of behavior and find new solutions to old problems.

Cultural expectations and social norms often shape our desires. We are taught from a young age what we should want and aspire to, based on the values and ideals of the society we live in. These expectations can be limiting, as they may not reflect our true passions and desires.

On the other hand, our desires may also be shaped by our imaginations and fantasies, which can sometimes be disconnected from reality. While it is important to dream and imagine new possibilities, it is also important to ground our desires in the reality of our lives and the world. In theater, we refer to the reality that shapes the story as "the given circumstances." Likewise, in real life, we have to maintain awareness of the given circumstances while still imagining what else could be possible.

When we can clearly envision a future that differs from our current reality, we are more likely to take action to make that future a reality. We are more willing to take risks, to try new things, and to push through obstacles and setbacks. Living a fulfilling life requires a balance between our cultural expectations and our personal imagination. There is no single blueprint for living, and each of us must find our own way to navigate the complex landscape of our desires and aspirations. By embracing our unique passions and aspirations, while also staying grounded in the reality of our lives, we can find a path towards greater fulfillment and meaning.

There are many ways to develop the imagination, such as through creative writing, visualization exercises, or simply engaging in play and exploration. Actors often use various techniques to stimulate their imagination, such as improvisation, sensory exploration, and emotional recall. By practicing these techniques, they can expand their range of emotional expression, develop a greater sense of spontaneity and authenticity, and tap into their own unique creativity and imagination. And we can use these techniques even if we aren't on stage. Wouldn't your life benefit from deeper emotional expression, more authenticity, and more vigorous creativity?

Another great exercise is called stream-of-consciousness writing, which is a technique that involves writing continuously without worrying about grammar, spelling, or punctuation. The goal is to allow your thoughts to flow freely onto paper or screen. This technique can help to develop imagination by allowing the writer to access their subconscious and explore their thoughts and feelings in a more spontaneous and intuitive way.

To practice stream-of-consciousness writing, find a quiet place where you can be alone with your thoughts. Set a timer for a specific amount of time, say 10 or 15 minutes. Then write whatever comes to mind, without worrying about making sense or being coherent. Write about your day, your feelings, your dreams, your fears, your fantasies - anything that pops into your mind. If you get stuck, just keep writing the same word or phrase until a new thought comes to you.

The key to this exercise is to keep writing without stopping or pausing to edit or correct. Don't worry about making sense or having a clear structure. Just let your thoughts flow onto the page. After you finish writing, take a moment to read over what you wrote. You may be surprised at what comes out when you allow yourself to write without inhibitions. Use this exercise as a tool for self-reflection and creative exploration, and don't be afraid to revisit your stream of consciousness writing to mine it for insights or inspiration.

To be or not to be?

Theater has a long history of exploring what I call "soul questions." By creating compelling narratives and complex characters, theater explores the depths of the human experience and asks questions that go beyond the confines of our everyday lives. Through theater, we can confront our fears, grapple with our doubts, and gain new insights into the nature of our existence.

Soul questions are deep, existential, and go beyond the surface-level concerns of everyday life. They are questions that probe the very nature of our being and our place in the world. Some examples of soul questions include:

- *What is the meaning of life?*

- *Who am I?*

- *What is my purpose?*

- *What happens after we die?*

- *What is the nature of reality?*

- *To be or not to be?*

These questions are difficult to answer, and they can be unsettling or even frightening to contemplate. However, they are also central to the human experience and can be—if you face them bravely—a source of inspiration.

Theater can also provide a space for communal exploration and reflection. By bringing people together to share in a theatrical experience, theater creates a sense of connection and shared purpose that can be difficult to find in our increasingly fragmented and isolated world. Through theater, we can engage in a collective exploration of the soul questions that are central to our lives, and we can find support and understanding from others who are on a similar journey.

By exploring the deepest, most fundamental questions of human existence, theater has the power to inspire, challenge, and transform us in profound ways. It can remind us of our shared humanity and our collective quest for meaning and purpose, and it can help us navigate. Don't force the complex and often confusing terrain of our inner lives.

That said, you don't have to go to the theater or practice theater to explore the idea of soul questions. Here's an example of an exercise that can help you connect with your soul:

1. Find a quiet and comfortable space where you won't be disturbed.

2. Take a few deep breaths to relax your body and mind.

3. Close your eyes and bring your attention to your breath. Observe your breath as it goes in and out.

4. Ask yourself a soul question that resonates with you. Here are a few examples: *What is my purpose in life? What are my core values? What brings me joy and fulfillment? What do I want to be remembered for?*

5. Allow yourself to sit with the question for a few minutes. Don't force an answer or come up with a solution. Instead, just observe your thoughts and feelings as they arise.

6. When you feel ready, take a few deep breaths and slowly open your eyes.

7. Take a few moments to reflect on what came up for you during the exercise. You may want to journal about your experience or simply sit with your thoughts for a few minutes.

You are the Protagonist

Whether you are aware of it, you are the protagonist of your life. You are the central character in your story, and the choices you make and the actions you take shape the plot of your life.

It's important to recognize that you are the protagonist of your life because it puts you in the driver's seat. You have the power to make choices and take action towards the things you want to achieve, rather than simply being a passive observer. You may even feel sometimes that you are the antagonist in your life, fated to lose. Using theater to understand these roles can help you release the idea that you are the "enemy" and embrace the agency and freedom that comes from being your own protagonist.

Of course, there are external factors that can influence your life and the choices you make, such as societal expectations, economic constraints, and the actions of others. But ultimately, you have the power to choose how you respond to these external factors and to shape your own experience.

Here's an exercise to explore being the protagonist of your life through the Hero's Journey. [2]

---

2. To download a free PDF copy of this exercise, visit http s://atomica-arts.com/the-heros-journey/

1. Take a few minutes to reflect on your own life journey so far. Think about a significant challenge or obstacle you faced or are currently facing.

2. Identify yourself as the main character in your own hero's journey. What is your main goal in this journey?

3. Identify the obstacle or challenge that you must overcome to achieve your goal.

4. Consider who or what can help you along the way. This could be a person, a community, a belief, or anything else that can provide support and guidance.

5. Think about coping with the obstacle. What strategies have you used or can you use to overcome it?

6. Finally, reflect on how your hero's journey ends. Does it end with you achieving your goal, or is the journey ongoing? What have you learned from the experience?

By using the structure of the Hero's Journey, you can explore your own journey as the protagonist of your life and gain insights into how you can navigate the challenges and obstacles that come your way. When you recognize you are the protagonist of your life, you can take ownership of your experiences and take intentional action towards creating the life you want to live.

Many people live their lives passively, allowing external circumstances or other people's expectations to dictate the direction of their lives. They may feel like they are merely going through the motions, rather than actively shaping their own destinies. Becoming the protagonist of our lives means breaking out of this pattern and taking an active role in creating a more intentional and fulfilling life journey.

One way to do this is by setting clear goals and taking concrete steps to achieve them. By setting goals, you give yourself a clear sense of direction and purpose, and you can work towards achieving those goals with intention and focus. This can help you feel more in control of your own life and to create a sense of momentum and progress.

Another way to become the protagonist of your life is by taking ownership of your own stories. You can reflect on your life experiences in a way that empowers you rather than holds you back. By reframing your stories in a positive light, you can create a sense of agency and control over your own life.

Step into the spotlight of your life and become the protagonist of your own remarkable story. Embrace the transformative power of theater and storytelling, igniting a flame within that empowers you to navigate your journey with empathy, openness, and a commitment to making a positive impact. No longer be a mere spectator in life, swayed by external forces or others' expectations. Break free from the chains of passivity and take charge of your destiny.

Your narrative is yours to shape.

Lila

The Art of Becoming the Protagonist

A Holistic Approach to the Play of Life

When I resigned from my last full-time job to start my business as an independent consultant, I looked back at my journey. A mix of nervousness and excitement accompanied this decision because it represented a significant change in my life. Becoming an entrepreneur created a whirlwind of emotions as I embraced the challenges and possibilities that lay ahead.

In that pivotal moment, Steve Jobs' words echoed in my life. He had wisely said that we cannot connect the dots looking forward; only in retrospect can we piece them together. Like him, I trusted that every experience, every pursuit, each teacher certification, and all the tools I had gained, seemingly unrelated at first glance, would eventually intertwine and reveal a profound connection.

One fateful day, a revelation struck me like a lightning bolt - my passion for theater had beautifully interwoven with the tranquil essence of meditation and the profound wisdom of Ayurveda, all coming together to set the stage for the art of becoming the protagonist of my life. At that moment, Atomica Arts was born.

At different points in my life, the Arts of Observing Life, Ourselves, and Human Actions found their way to me, each contributing its unique essence to my journey.

The stage has always felt like a sanctuary, a place where I could shed inhibitions and step into the shoes of a myriad of characters. The allure of storytelling and the ability to evoke emotions in others fueled my passion, leading me to embrace theater as an integral part of my life. With each performance, I discovered new facets of myself, exploring the depths of human emotions and the complexities of relationships. Theater became a mirror, reflecting the human experience back at me, and in those moments of vulnerability, I found strength and authenticity.

As life unfolded, meditation became my refuge, a tranquil oasis amid the chaos of daily existence. Amidst the hustle and bustle, I sought solace in the stillness, seeking answers within my mind and heart. Meditation became a gateway to self-awareness, allowing me to observe my thoughts and emotions with clarity and without judgment. Through this practice, I discovered inner peace, resilience, and a newfound sense of purpose.

And then, like a beautiful tapestry finally coming into view, Ayurveda stepped onto the stage of my life. A chance encounter with this ancient healing tradition introduced me to a world of interconnectedness where the elements of nature danced in harmony within and around me. The holistic approach of Ayurveda resonated deeply, as I realized that the mind, body, and spirit were intrinsically linked, and nurturing one meant nurturing the whole.

Atomica Arts became a manifestation of the interconnectedness I had discovered in my life. At its core, it is a business that offers workshops, classes, and personalized sessions to guide individuals on their transformative journeys. By interweaving Ayurveda, meditation, and theater, Atomica Arts empowers individuals to embrace their vulnerabilities, step into their authenticity, and take charge of their own narratives within the Play of Life.

Lila

The idea of Lila, from the Vedas, is the concept that the universe and all of life is a grand play or game, also referred to as the "Play of God," "Divine Play," or "Leela." It suggests that the universe and all living beings are actors in this play, and that the ultimate goal is to understand and transcend the illusion of the material world.

This notion is like the idea of being the protagonist of your own life in the sense that it emphasizes the importance of agency and self-determination. Both concepts suggest that you have the power to shape your own life and determine your own destiny.

There is, however, a key difference between the two ideas. The concept of Lila emphasizes that the universe and all of life are an illusion, and that the goal is to transcend it. In contrast, the idea of being the protagonist focuses on you having the power to shape your own life and determine your destiny within the reality of the material world.

Additionally, the concept of Lila is rooted in the spiritual and philosophical tradition of the Vedas, whereas the idea of being the protagonist of your own life is a more modern, secular concept. The former is more oriented toward finding the ultimate meaning, and the latter is more oriented toward finding practical ways to empower yourself.

My offering in this book is that you can fuse these two ideas. While the concept of Lila reminds you of the fleeting nature of everything and urges you to find happiness and detachment in the present moment, being the protagonist of your own life requires active engagement in the material realm.

I believe it is important for you to pursue goals and dreams, to build relationships with others, and to contribute to society. By balancing detachment and engagement, you can appreciate the present moment while also taking the actions necessary to shape your own life.

Cultivating a holistic approach to living that embraces both spiritual growth and worldly pursuits will allow you to live with purpose, meaning, and fulfillment.

Basically, your Play of Life is not yet written. Or rather, you write a few more lines each day. If you focus solely on the destination—on the end of your play—you risk missing out on the joys and opportunities that the journey itself presents. It is the moments of self-discovery, the people you meet, the obstacles you overcome, and the victories—large or small—you achieve along the way that truly make your play meaningful and rewarding. I believe that by being mindful and present in these moments, the attainment of your destination will be even more gratifying.

Just like in a play, there are different roles that you can choose to take on in life, and you can experiment with different ways of being and interacting with others. You can also learn from the experiences and challenges that you encounter, and use these as opportunities for growth and self-discovery.

Through the wisdom of Ayurveda, you can observe the interconnection of all things and recognize that your well-being is intricately linked to the well-being of the world around you. Meditation can offer you the ability to observe your true self, free from the constraints of ego and self-judgment, allowing you to take part in life's dance with authenticity and grace. Theatre invites you to observe the myriad roles you play and to embrace the vulnerability of being human, acknowledging that every character in this divine play holds significance.

The Play of Life involves an element of creativity and spontaneity as you navigate the unexpected twists and turns that come your way. You can approach life with a sense of playfulness and curiosity, and be open to new experiences and opportunities for growth.

However, the Play of Life involves more than fun and games; it requires taking responsibility for your choices, being mindful of their impact on others and the world, and navigating consequences with care while embracing the role of the protagonist.

It is crucial to recognize that other people are also the protagonists of their own lives, charting their unique paths and making meaningful decisions that shape their destinies. Recognizing the significance of every individual's story and our interconnectedness fosters a deeper sense of responsibility towards the well-being of others and the world we share.

Ultimately, the art of becoming the protagonist in the Play of Life is about finding a balance between playfulness and responsibility, creativity and discipline, and spontaneity and mindfulness. By approaching life as a kind of play or game, you can cultivate a sense of joy, curiosity, and adventure, and live a more fulfilling and meaningful life.

The Power of the Five Senses

As I delved into creating my work at Atomica Arts to guide individuals to be present and truly engaged in the journey of life, a profound revelation emerged - the incredible power of our five senses, as taught in the ancient wisdom of Ayurveda, the introspective practice of Meditation, and the transformative world of Theater. These three pillars, seemingly distinct, converge at the intersectionality of the human experience, emphasizing the significance of our senses in shaping our realities.

Ayurveda recognizes the vital role our senses play in understanding the world. It teaches us to nurture and develop each sense through conscious living, allowing us to fully immerse in the richness of our experiences.

Meditation encourages us to be present in the moment, honing our awareness by attuning to our senses - the sights, sounds, smells, tastes, and tactile sensations that anchor us in the "now."

The profound connection between our senses and the art of Theater reveals itself in the portrayal of characters and emotions. Actors delve deep into their sensory experiences to embody the essence of their roles, enabling audiences to empathize and connect on a visceral level. Theater brings to life the nuances of human senses, bridging the gap between performer and spectator, and allowing everyone present to share in the collective experience.

By awakening your senses and harnessing their power, you can unlock the transformative potential of your journey. By embracing and refining your sensory perception, you can fully immerse yourself in the journey of life and become the architect of your destiny.

Amidst this celebration of the senses, I want to acknowledge those living with impaired senses. Being deaf or blind does not diminish one's ability to be the protagonist of their life's story. Far from it - individuals with impaired senses have exhibited extraordinary resilience, adaptability, and strength in navigating their paths. Deprived of one sense, the others can compensate, creating a new perspective on the world, demonstrating that being the protagonist is not defined solely by the functioning of our senses but by the spirit within.

The interplay between our senses offers a remarkable form of compensation. A blind person's sense of touch becomes more refined, enabling them to perceive the world with heightened sensitivity. Likewise, a deaf individual's eyes become attuned to subtle visual cues and expressions that escape others. This reciprocity among our senses reinforces the notion that being the protagonist of our lives is not contingent on any single sense, but on the totality of our being.

The five senses - sight, hearing, touch, taste, and smell - are the primary way that we experience and interact with the world. Each of these senses provides us with unique information about our environment, and together they allow us to form a rich and complex understanding of the world.

Sight allows us to perceive visual information, such as colors, shapes, and patterns, and gives us a sense of spatial awareness. Hearing allows us to perceive sounds and speech, and provides us with information about the location and movement of objects in our environment. Touch provides us with information about the texture, temperature, and pressure of objects, and allows us to perceive physical sensations such as pain, pleasure, and pressure. Taste and smell allow us to perceive and distinguish different flavors and scents, and can be important for detecting potential dangers such as spoiled food or smoke.

The five senses are not only important for our physical survival, but they also play a critical role in our emotional and social experiences, all of which are essential in our journey of becoming the protagonist. For example, the sound of a loved one's voice, the taste of a favorite food, or the feel of a warm embrace can all evoke powerful emotional responses and contribute to our sense of well-being.

During the hushed silence enveloping the world amidst the COVID-19 pandemic lockdown, an extraordinary revelation dawned on me. Immersed in the practices of Ayurveda, Meditation, and Theater, seeking solace and understanding amid the uncertainty and challenges of the times, I unearthed the transformative power these disciplines had on my senses.

A still outside world amplified the resonance of my inner being and the different ways I could become aware of my senses. This powerful realization illuminated the resilience of the human spirit and its boundless capacity to assume the role of protagonists in our own lives, even amid the most challenging of times.

Using Your Senses as the Protagonist

Ayurveda emphasizes the importance of paying attention to your senses and using them to maintain balance and promote well-being. Meditation teaches us to observe our senses without judgment or attachment. Theater can provide valuable insights into the workings of the senses and how we can use them to better understand ourselves and others. By becoming more aware of our senses, we can learn to notice when they are becoming overwhelmed or overstimulated, and take steps to bring them back into balance.

Use the list below to give you some practical ideas of how to use your senses in your protagonist's journey to feel more present, balanced, and create positive sensory memories.

Sound

- Listen to pleasing music.

- Sing a favorite melody.

- Recite meaningful mantras.

- Take part in inspiring discussions.

- Enjoy the sounds of nature.

- Follow the sound of your breath.

- Engage in guided meditation sessions with soothing audio tracks.

- Reduce or avoid exposure to unnecessary, displeasing or aggravating sounds.

Touch

- Perform a daily self-oil massage or receive massages.

- Give and receive hugs.

- Soak in a warm bath.

- Wear comfortable clothes and natural skin products.

- Walk in the rain.*

- Walk barefoot on natural surfaces and experience grounding.

- Move your body and engage in activities that involve tactile sensations, such as pottery or gardening.

- Reduce or avoid synthetic fibers, skin products with artificial ingredients, exposure to extreme temperatures, and any uncomfortable contact.

*Note that our senses also intertwine and collaborate in a symphony of experiences. In this example, as we walk in the rain, we hear the soft sound of raindrops on the ground, and we smell the fresh, invigorating scent of wet air and grass. It all comes together to create a wonderful experience that makes a simple walk in the rain feel even more special.

Sight

- Surround yourself with images that are pleasant to you.

- Watch beautiful sunrises or sunsets to connect with nature's beauty.

- Expose your eyes to natural light.

- Dress in and decorate your space with colors that balance you.

- Visit art galleries or museums to appreciate visual expressions of creativity.

- Experience your inner vision.

- Engage in visual art forms like drawing, painting, or photography.

- Reduce or avoid harsh light, negative or unpleasant images, eyestrain, excessive visual stimulation, and exposure to high heat or dry conditions.

Taste

- Nourish all levels of your being with satisfying tastes.

- Drink room temperature water.

- Include the six tastes (sour, pungent, bitter, sweet, salty, astringent) in each meal.

- Use herbs and spices.

- Experiment with different cuisines and flavors from diverse cultures.

- Involve all of your senses while eating. Try eating in silence.

- Avoid eating while in a hurry or when upset.

- Avoid eating artificial, processed, or chemical foods.

Smell

- Include enjoyable aromas in your daily routine.*

- Diffuse essential oils into the air.

- Keep fresh flowers in your home and office or plant an herb garden.

- Spend time in natural environments like forests or gardens to enjoy the natural scents.

- Use naturally fragranced health and home products.

- Receive aromatherapy treatments.

- Savor the smell of fresh food.

- Reduce or avoid unpleasant odors with negative associations, artificial fragrances, and mold.

* It's essential for individuals to explore and discover aromas that resonate with their unique preferences and bring them joy. Two popular choices that often have widespread appeal are lavender, known for its calming and soothing effects, and citrus scents like orange and lemon, which offer invigorating and uplifting properties, providing a diverse range of options to elevate mood and reduce stress.

Awareness is Freedom

As I sat at my desk, reflecting on the journey that led me to write this book, a moment of profound realization came together—the art of observing in Ayurveda, Meditation, and Theater is not a mere coincidence. Each discipline offers a unique perspective on the practice of mindful observation, and together, they form a comprehensive framework for cultivating heightened awareness.

In my journey of becoming the protagonist of my life, I have learned that awareness is not a distant and elusive state of mind, but the natural outcome of deliberate observation. Through Ayurveda, I learned to observe the elements within and around me—the tastes of food, the sensations in my body, the rhythms of nature. Meditation taught me to observe the fluctuations of my thoughts and emotions, to be present with the breath, and to embrace each passing moment without judgment. And finally, Theater encouraged me to observe the intricacies of human behavior, to step into the shoes of others, and to experience life through different perspectives.

Becoming the protagonist of my life has brought me a sense of liberation and expanded possibilities. Ayurveda, Meditation, and Theater have taught me to pay attention to the present moment with a non-judgmental attitude. Through these art forms, I can say that I have developed a deeper understanding of myself and the world around me. The more mindful and self-aware I become, the more I see new possibilities for growth and transformation that were previously hidden from my view.

This profound realization I now offer to you: to be truly aware, you don't need to embark on an extraordinary quest or seek an elusive state of being. The key is in the simplicity of daily observation—engaging your senses mindfully in all that you do. Each moment offers an opportunity to observe, learn, and grow, and these three disciplines are the powerful lenses through which you can view the world.

Awareness is not an abstract concept but a tangible, accessible state that can be nurtured through the daily work of observing.

As you finish reading these pages, I hope you will come to recognize the beauty and significance of your own sensory experiences. I hope you embrace the wisdom of Ayurveda, the serenity of Meditation, and the empathy of Theater as powerful tools for cultivating a life of heightened awareness. By engaging your five senses with intention and presence, you can unlock the secrets of your journey and become the conscious, empowered protagonist of your own story.

As you embark on this journey of self-reflection, imagine yourself as both the spectator and the protagonist in the grand Play of Life. Just like attending a theatrical performance, you are both aware of the make-believe nature of the world around you and yet emotionally immersed in its unfolding drama.

This delicate tension between detachment and engagement is the key to unlocking the gates of heightened awareness.

Consider the following ways to bring more awareness into your life.

Cultivate a Sense of Playfulness

After all, to be the protagonist in your life is to be an actor in a play. Approaching tasks and activities with a spirit of joy and spontaneity can help to reduce stress, increase creativity, and improve overall well-being. Here are some practical examples of how to cultivate playfulness:

- Play a game or sport that you enjoy

- Try a new hobby or activity just for fun

- Approach a challenging task with a playful attitude

- Find humor in everyday situations and laugh at yourself

- Spend time with playful people who make you laugh

Embrace Impermanence

After all, a play always comes to an end. The lights go black, the curtain comes down, the actors take their bow, and everyone goes home. Recognizing the impermanent nature of everything can help to reduce attachment and cultivate a sense of detachment from material possessions, relationships, and even our own sense of self. Here are some practical examples of how to embrace impermanence:

- Practice decluttering and letting go of things you no longer need

- Spend time in nature and observe the changing seasons

- Reflect on the impermanence of your own body and the life cycle of all living things

- Practice non-attachment in relationships by letting go of expectations and appreciating the present moment

- Practice mindfulness to cultivate awareness of the impermanent nature of thoughts and emotions

Appreciate the Beauty of Existence

After all, in a play, the director and designers have worked together for months to make every costume, every light cue, every sound effect look and sound as beautiful as possible. Appreciating the beauty and complexity of the world around us can bring a sense of wonder and awe, and improve overall well-being. Here are some practical examples of how to appreciate the beauty of existence:

- Spend time in nature, such as hiking, camping, or gardening

- Listen to music or attend a live performance

- Visit art galleries or museums

- Spend time with loved ones and appreciate their unique qualities

- Practice gratitude for the blessings in your life

Recognize the Illusory Nature of Reality

After all, nothing about a play is "real." That set is just painted wood. Those actors have those lines memorized, and next month they'll be playing a different character. Recognizing the illusory nature of reality can help to see through the illusions of the ego and material world and cultivate a deeper sense of awareness and wisdom. Here are some practical examples of how to recognize the illusory nature of reality:

- Practice mindfulness and observe thoughts and emotions without judgment

- Question your assumptions and beliefs about the world

- Explore different perspectives and philosophies

- Practice self-inquiry and examine the nature of the self

- Reflect on the impermanent nature of everything around you

ENGAGE IN SPIRITUAL PRACTICE

Throughout history, theater emerged from religious festivals, and even today there are rituals most plays follow, from ticket buying to curtain speeches to overtures to curtain calls. Every actor has their own superstitions and warm-ups. Engaging in spiritual practices can help cultivate a deeper sense of understanding and wisdom. Here are some practical examples of how to engage in spiritual practice:

- Practice meditation or prayer regularly

- Attend a religious or spiritual community gathering

- Read spiritual texts or books

- Practice yoga or other physical practices that connect mind, body, and spirit

- Engage in acts of service or volunteer work that align with spiritual values

Be the Protagonist

Living as the protagonist requires taking charge of your life and actively shaping the narrative you wish to create. Define your objectives. Make choices that align with your principles. Hold yourself accountable for the outcomes of those decisions. And you will find yourself on your own Hero's Journey.

But also understand: it is a *process*. You can't just meditate once and wake up the next day as the protagonist. I work every day toward becoming the protagonist of my life. Although I am not flawless in fulfilling the roles I play, I strive to do so with sincerity, moment by moment. Here is what daily embodying this approach entails:

AS AN INDEPENDENT CONSULTANT, I strive to embody this approach in all aspects of my life, continuously seeking growth and improvement while maintaining sincerity and mindfulness in each role I play.

AS A WIFE, I actively strive to improve my relationship with my husband by regularly communicating my needs, expressing gratitude for his contributions, and making time for quality moments together. This can look like setting aside dedicated date nights, expressing appreciation for the small things he does, and openly discussing any issues or concerns that arise in a respectful and constructive manner. In conflicts, I take responsibility for my part and work toward finding solutions that benefit both of us.

As a parent, my top priority is my children's well-being. I prioritize this by setting clear boundaries that promote their safety and growth, providing emotional support and guidance, and modeling healthy behaviors. This can include things like listening actively to their concerns, setting rules and expectations, and being open and honest about my own struggles and challenges. When I make mistakes or hurt their feelings, I take responsibility for my actions and apologize sincerely.

As a teaching artist, I am committed to constantly improving my skills by seeking feedback, reflecting on my practices, and continuing to learn. This involves attending workshops and conferences, reading, and taking part in online learning communities. I also strive to create a positive and inclusive environment where everyone feels valued and supported.

As a citizen, I believe it is my responsibility to be an engaged and active member of my community. This means taking ownership of my role in creating a better society by participating in local events, volunteering with community organizations, and advocating for causes that align with my values. This might involve attending town hall meetings or participating in peaceful protests or rallies. I also strive to be informed about current events and to engage in respectful and constructive dialogue with others who may have different perspectives.

Although I strive to practice the various habits and roles mentioned, I must admit that I don't always do them perfectly. Being the protagonist of my life is an ongoing journey that requires constant effort and growth. Writing about these practices helps me to remain accountable and motivated to continue working on them. As the saying goes, we often teach what we most need to learn ourselves. Teaching you reminds me I need to walk the talk and continuously work on embodying these principles in my daily life.

And now... it's your turn! By becoming the protagonist of your own life, you can live authentically and free yourself from any expectations or limitations imposed by others. You can stay true to your values and live a purposeful life.

Start by becoming more aware. You may choose to incorporate Ayurveda, Meditation, or Theater into your life, but ultimately it can be as simple as observing your thoughts, feelings, and actions throughout the day. Notice when you're on autopilot and make a conscious effort to take back control. Set goals and make plans to achieve them, and take action every day to move closer to your desired destination. It may not always be easy, but the rewards of living as the protagonist are worth it.

May Ayurveda nourish your body, Meditation calm your mind, and Theater awaken your soul, weaving a harmonious melody of awareness that dances through the tapestry of your life's unfolding masterpiece.

Acknowledgments

My journey of writing this book has been deeply transformative, filled with self-discovery and growth. I am truly grateful to everyone who played a crucial role in bringing this project to life. First and foremost, my heartfelt gratitude goes out to my parents, Hilario and Sonia, and my sister Ana Luiza, for their unwavering support throughout my life.

To my loving husband, Will, I want to express my love and gratitude for always having my back. And to my incredible children, Olivia and Leila, you are my greatest joy and the most significant source of inspiration in my life.

I am profoundly indebted to my book editor, Jason, whose keen eye and invaluable insights have shaped this manuscript into its best possible form.

To all the teachers and colleagues who have profoundly influenced my life and journey, your knowledge and wisdom have enriched my understanding of the world and left an indelible mark on the pages of this book.

Lastly, I extend my heartfelt appreciation to you, the readers of this book, for embarking on this transformative journey with me. I sincerely hope that the words within these pages inspire and empower you to embrace your own path as the protagonist of your life.

All my deep appreciation and love to you.

About Author

Maria is a Brazilian-born educator and artist, on a passionate mission to empower individuals to become the protagonists of their own lives. With extensive experience in theater, mindfulness, and cross-cultural engagement, she weaves together the transformative power of theater, Ayurveda, and meditation to guide others on a journey of self-discovery and well-being.

Maria's deep commitment to personal growth led her to become a certified Chopra Meditation teacher, Reiki Master, and Ayurvedic Health Counselor. Through her company, Atomica Arts, she pioneers the integration of mindfulness practices into her artistic and educational endeavors, nurturing creativity and fostering well-being through arts-based activities.

As a National Arts Integration Consultant, Maria excels in designing and implementing transformative residencies and workshops with a strong emphasis on theater, improvisation, mindfulness, social change, and mental health. Her remarkable contributions to the field of arts and education have garnered her recognition, including receiving the 2019 Arts Leadership Award from The Arts and Cultural Alliance of Sarasota County. Additionally, she was honored with the prestigious 2022 Appleton Arts Integration Award from the Sarasota Performing Arts Center Foundation.

To embark on a journey of empowerment, mindfulness, and creativity with Maria, visit her website at www.atomica-arts .com and discover the transformative possibilities she brings through her art, teaching, and holistic well-being practices.

Stories Take Flight
at Ibis Books

IBIS
B O O K S

The **IBIS** is sacred to Thoth, the Egyptian god of learning, inventor of writing, and scribe to the gods.

They are gregarious birds that live, travel, and breed in flocks.

And they are legendary for their courage.

ibis-books.com

www.ingramcontent.com/pod-product-compliance
Lightning Source LLC
Chambersburg PA
CBHW021647120626
46545CB00002B/737